Spectrum Response

Bridging the Gap Between Autism and First Responders

Author Joshua Creamer

Spectrum Response LLC product

This book is dedicated to my daughter, Lilian Creamer, my non-verbal angel who is special and unique in her own beautiful way. Lilian, you inspire me every single day with your strength, resilience, and the way you navigate a world that often struggles to understand you. Your light and spirit remind me why this work matters.

To all the autistic individuals out there, this book is also for you. It is my hope that it cultivates a greater understanding and bridges the gap between the autism spectrum and the world of first responders. Through this work, I aim to create awareness and equip those who serve with the knowledge to respond with compassion, patience, and insight. May this book be a step toward a future where everyone is seen, heard, and valued for who they truly are.

Spectrum Response: Bridging The Gap Between Autism And First Responders

© 2025 Joshua Creamer. All rights reserved.

No part of this book may be reproduced, stored in a retrieval system, or transmitted in any form or by any means, electronic, mechanical, photocopy, recording, or otherwise, without the prior written permission of the author, except for brief quotations used in critical reviews, scholarly works, or other non-commercial purposes where proper credit is given.

This book is intended for personal use only. Any unauthorized use, reproduction, or distribution of its contents may violate copyright, trademark, and other intellectual property laws.

The content and opinions expressed in this book are solely those of the author and do not necessarily reflect the views of any organizations with which the author is affiliated.

For permission requests, licensing inquiries, or any other questions, please contact: [spectrumresponsellc@gmail.com]

ISBN: 9798303086883   Independently published

Table of Contents

Prologue..5

Chapter 1: Understanding Autism Spectrum Disorder............................9

Chapter 2: Autism Across the Lifespan..48

Chapter 3: Strategies for Effective Communication..............................58

Chapter 4: Approach Techniques...84

Chapter 5: Interactions during a crisis..112

Chapter 6: Family dynamics and Caregiver Support............................148

Chapter 7: Collaboration with Autism Organizations..........................172

Chapter 8: Legal Considerations...202

Chapter 9: Every Call Counts, Why Training Never Stops.....................224

The Road Ahead: Embracing the Unknown...238

Prologue

As a decorated Law Enforcement Officer with ten years of experience and a father to an autistic child, I bring a unique perspective on community interactions and crisis management. My personal life has been profoundly shaped by my role as a parent to a stage 3 non-verbal autistic daughter, whom I love with all my heart. This combination of professional and personal experience has given me deep insights into the challenges faced by individuals on the autism spectrum and their families.

Through my journey, I have observed several strategies and approaches that can significantly improve interactions between first responders and individuals with autism. These strategies not only aid first responders in their responses but also provide parents with valuable tools for raising their children in a way that fosters understanding and communication. I believe that by sharing my insights, we can bridge the gap between first responders and the autism community, ensuring that both officers and families feel supported and empowered.

Having seen the importance of effective communication and empathy firsthand, I advocate for training programs that focus on understanding the unique behaviors and needs of individuals with autism. I aim to create an environment where first responders can respond appropriately and compassionately, ensuring the safety and well-being of all involved. Through collaboration, education, and open dialogue, we can enhance the lives of individuals with autism and build a more inclusive community for everyone.

The purpose of this book is to equip first responders with the knowledge and skills necessary to effectively respond to individuals with Autism Spectrum Disorder (ASD). With a deeper understanding of the unique challenges and characteristics associated with autism, first responders can improve the quality of their interactions and provide more effective assistance.

One critical outcome of this book is to provide a deeper understanding and ability to develop better communication. First responders will learn strategies to engage meaningfully with individuals on the spectrum, ensuring clear, respectful dialogue that accommodates different communication styles. This approach not only promotes mutual understanding but also helps build trust during interactions.

In addition, when implementing the techniques taught in this book responders will develop strategies to reduce anxiety in tense situations. By recognizing sensory sensitivities and behavioral cues, responders can implement calming strategies, creating an environment that minimizes stress and allows for smoother encounters.

Finally, the book emphasizes the importance of ensuring safety and dignity for all involved. Responders will have an understanding on how to prioritize the well-being and rights of individuals with autism by maintaining a respectful and supportive approach. This focus on empathy and care is essential in promoting positive outcomes and building community trust.

This book aims to provide practical strategies, resources, and insights that will help first responders navigate interactions with individuals on the autism spectrum. By doing so, it seeks to promote more positive outcomes for both the individuals and the community, enhancing overall public safety and trust in first responders.

Chapter 1

Understanding Autism Spectrum Disorder

I want you to take a moment and imagine what it was like when you had your first child. Whether you've experienced parenthood or not, picture that feeling, the joy, the excitement, the overwhelming sense of love and possibility. Imagine all the things you were eager to teach them, the adventures you dreamed of sharing, and the places you couldn't wait to take them. There's an inherent hope that as parents, we will give our children more than we ever had, provide them with opportunities, and help them reach their fullest potential.

Now, imagine taking all of that and watching it shift. Not because you won't be able to do any of those things, but because the way you do them will need to change drastically. The world you once imagined now requires a new set of lenses, because your child has been diagnosed with autism.

I vividly remember the day our lives shifted when our daughter was diagnosed with autism. In an instant, everything changed. We found ourselves on uncharted ground, unsure of where to go, what to do, or how to navigate this new world. The path ahead was unclear, and the dream we had for our daughter felt like it had been turned upside down. But it wasn't the end of the dream, it was the beginning of a new chapter, one where we would learn to redefine what it means to support, nurture, and love our child. Before that moment, every day was filled with uncertainty, endless questions, and conflicting answers from those around us. We heard different theories from doctors, teachers, and even family and friends. Some insisted we were overreacting, brushing off our concerns and labeling our daughter's behaviors as "normal," while others subtly blamed our parenting. The weight of these comments made us doubt ourselves, leaving us to wonder if we were doing something wrong or imagining problems that weren't really there.

    But on the day of her diagnosis, something unexpected happened for me. I felt a strange sense of peace, almost like a weight was lifted. Yes, the diagnosis was overwhelming, and yes, it came with new challenges. But it was also a moment of clarity, a confirmation that all those feelings and observations we'd had were real, not just in our heads. This wasn't an end; it was the beginning of a journey, one where we could finally get her the support she deserved.

My wife, on the other hand, struggled in a different way. While I felt relieved, she felt the weight of that diagnosis in a way that I couldn't fully understand. It wasn't that she loved our daughter any less; if anything, her love drove her fears. She wondered, what comes next? How do we help her grow and thrive? The road ahead seemed like a mountain with no map to guide us.

As husband and wife, we became each other's strength, even though we coped in opposite ways. My peace allowed me to research, to ask questions, and to start understanding autism as best I could. My wife, meanwhile, leaned on me, processing at her own pace, bringing her unwavering compassion to the table. Together, we embraced a new mission: learning how to navigate this world with our daughter and figuring out what "understanding autism" really meant for us as a family.

Autism Spectrum Disorder (ASD) is a neurodevelopmental disorder that affects communication, behavior, and social interaction. It is called a "spectrum" because individuals with autism can exhibit a wide range of symptoms and varying levels of severity. Some individuals may require significant support, while others may be highly independent and will function in society on their own.

Importance of Understanding Autism for first responders

Understanding autism is crucial for first responders for several reasons. Autism Spectrum Disorder (ASD) has been steadily increasing in recent years. According to current statistics, approximately 1 in 36 children is diagnosed with autism and that number continues to rise, a figure that reflects growing awareness and improved diagnostic practices. This rise means that encounters between law enforcement, fire fighters, paramedics, even calls to dispatchers and individuals on the spectrum are becoming more common.

Understanding the prevalence of autism is essential for first responders for several important reasons. As more individuals with autism participate in everyday activities, first responders are increasingly likely to encounter them in a variety of contexts. These interactions may occur during routine checks, public disturbances, or emergency situations, making it critical for first responders to be prepared to respond appropriately.

Being informed about the prevalence of autism also enhances first responders ability to recognize signs of the condition during interactions. With greater awareness, first responders can tailor their responses to meet the unique needs of individuals with autism, using more sensitive and effective communication strategies. This approach can prevent misunderstandings and de-escalate situations that might otherwise lead to unnecessary conflict.

Additionally, as society becomes more aware of autism, communities are engaging in deeper discussions about inclusivity and support for individuals with disabilities. Law enforcement's understanding and empathy toward these issues can play a crucial role in strengthening community relations. By demonstrating a commitment to inclusivity, first responders create trust and cooperation, contributing to safer and more supportive communities for all.

By equipping first responders with knowledge about the increasing prevalence of autism, agencies can prepare them to respond effectively and compassionately, ensuring the safety and dignity of individuals on the spectrum.

Individuals with Autism Spectrum Disorder (ASD) often experience unique communication challenges that can significantly impact their interactions with law enforcement. Recognizing and understanding these barriers is essential for promoting effective communication and minimizing misunderstandings. First responders who adjust their approach can create safer, more positive encounters and reduce the likelihood of conflict.

One common challenge is verbal communication. Some individuals with autism may have delayed speech or may be non-verbal, relying on alternative methods such as gestures, picture cards, or communication devices. First responders need to exercise patience and be prepared to adapt their communication style to accommodate these methods. Additionally, many individuals with autism interpret language literally, which can lead to confusion when idioms, metaphors, or slang are used. Clear, direct language free of jargon is essential to prevent miscommunication.

Echolalia, or the repetition of phrases or questions previously heard, presents another challenge. This behavior may not always reflect the individual's current thoughts or feelings, so first responders must avoid misinterpreting it as defiance or a lack of cooperation. Recognizing echolalia helps first responders respond appropriately without making assumptions about the individual's level of understanding.

Social cues can also be difficult for individuals with autism to interpret. They may struggle to recognize facial expressions, tone of voice, or body language, which can lead to misunderstandings in high-pressure situations. First responders should be mindful of their own non-verbal cues and maintain a calm and neutral demeanor to help reduce anxiety.

Believe it or not, many parents who care for someone on the autism spectrum live with a profound fear of what might happen if law enforcement is called to respond to their child. For many, this fear is so pervasive that they maintain a list of people they would call first, such as friends, neighbors, or therapists, before considering calling the police. This hesitation isn't necessarily born out of a lack of appreciation for law enforcement but rather a lack of trust, rooted in past experiences or stories they've heard from others. I myself have a list of people I plan on calling before I would ever consider calling the police, and I'm a police officer. But still, my understanding of the needs of my daughter is so much greater than any other law enforcement officer in the world, and each parent knows that, which is why most parents will call friends, family or therapists for help before calling the police. Understanding that many of the times we are dispatched to an autistic child, we are usually a last and final resort, or there is a threat against human life.

Throughout my career, I have encountered countless parents who shared this fear with me. They would express relief and gratitude that I was the one who responded, recounting previous encounters with other officers who, in their words, had treated them with indifference or misunderstanding, leaving them feeling alienated and judged. These parents often conveyed their ultimate fear, that calling law enforcement might end tragically, with their child being harmed or even killed because an officer misinterpreted their behavior as a threat.

As someone who has served in law enforcement, I know firsthand that the vast majority of officers enter this profession to make a difference. We choose this path because we believe in service, in protecting others, and in being there during moments of crisis. However, this noble intention is often overshadowed in the public eye by the actions of a few who make the news, tarnishing the trust we work so hard to build.

The reality is that many parents of children on the autism spectrum fear that law enforcement or first responders won't understand their child's unique needs. They worry we won't recognize that what might appear to be defiance or aggression is often a response to overwhelming stimuli, confusion, or an inability to communicate effectively. High-stress environments only exacerbate these challenges. For individuals with autism, loud noises, flashing lights, or sudden changes can lead to sensory overload, making it even harder for them to process or respond in expected ways.

For first responders, understanding these realities is crucial. By recognizing these sensory triggers and adjusting our approach, minimizing noise, maintaining calm tones, and providing clear, structured instructions; we can create an environment that guides trust rather than fear. When parents see that we understand and respect their child's needs, we have the opportunity to bridge the gap between apprehension and reassurance. It is only through empathy, training, and a commitment to continuous learning that we can truly serve the communities that depend on us.

By recognizing these communication barriers, first responders can modify their strategies to provide clearer dialogue and build rapport, ultimately reducing the likelihood of conflict and enhancing the overall interaction.

Pain Tolerance:

There are many things first responders need to be aware of when it comes to interacting with individuals on the autism spectrum. One critical aspect, often overlooked but with potentially severe consequences, is pain tolerance. Many individuals with autism exhibit a much higher pain tolerance than neurotypical individuals, a phenomenon that has been widely observed and documented. This heightened threshold for pain can pose significant health risks, as injuries or medical issues that typically cause intense discomfort may not elicit the expected response, delaying critical care or attention.

I'll never forget the day my daughter broke her arm. I was at work, and my wife called to explain what had happened. My daughter had jumped off her bed and walked into the living room, holding her arm and simply saying, "Ow." There were no tears, no screaming, no signs of the intense pain one would expect from a broken arm. What alarmed us even more was that she continued to stim by smacking her injured arm against the wall, laughing, and still saying, "Ow." Knowing her high pain tolerance, this subtle complaint was enough for us to realize something was seriously wrong. When I got home, we took her to the doctor, where X-rays confirmed her arm was indeed broken.

After the doctor applied a cast from her wrist to her elbow, we thought the situation was resolved. But just two days later, she had physically removed the cast. We had to return to the doctor to get a new one, this time extending from her wrist all the way above her elbow to prevent her from slipping it off again. Thankfully, the doctor understood our challenges and didn't charge us for the second visit. However, not every family is met with such understanding, and the financial strain of situations like this can be overwhelming.

Financial Hardship:

This brings me to another often-unspoken aspect of raising a child on the spectrum: the financial toll. The cost of raising a child with autism can be staggering, far beyond what many families are prepared for. I vividly remember one particularly challenging year when my daughter would eat nothing but Little Caesars pizza. Not just any pizza, it had to be pepperoni pizza, which she would carefully deconstruct, removing the pepperoni to eat only the cheese and crust. If we bought a plain cheese pizza, she refused to touch it. That year alone, we spent nearly $5,000 on pizzas because it was the only food she would eat consistently. The financial strain from this was difficult enough, but it didn't stop there.

Therapy costs add another layer of financial hardship. Many Applied Behavior Analysis (ABA) therapy services cost between $4,500 and $5,500 per month. These therapies are often critical for the development and well-being of individuals on the spectrum, but their cost is prohibitive for many families. Then there are additional items required to ensure the safety and comfort of the child. For example, my daughter's psychologist prescribed a specialized "cubby bed" for her, a safe and enclosed sleep environment. The average cost of a cubby bed is around $10,000, yet our insurance refused to cover it, leaving us to figure out how to pay for it ourselves.

And the expenses don't stop there. The list of needs continues to grow, from specialized equipment to dietary accommodations to therapy tools, and more. These ongoing costs can devastate families, both financially and emotionally. As first responders, it's critical to understand these challenges. The worst thing we can say to a family struggling to provide for their loved one on the spectrum is, "Just get them the help they need." Most families are already doing everything in their power to provide that help, but the financial burden makes it nearly impossible to achieve without sacrifices that affect every aspect of their lives.

Characteristics of Autism

Individuals with autism may display a variety of characteristics, which can include: **Social Interaction Challenges, Communication Difficulties, Repetitive Behaviors and Restricted Interests, Sensory Sensitivities, and Cognitive Profiles.**

Social Interaction Challenges:

Difficulty understanding social cues: Individuals with autism often struggle to interpret non-verbal signals such as body language, facial expressions, and tone of voice. This can lead to misunderstandings in social situations, making it challenging for them to navigate interactions. For example, they may not recognize when someone is being sarcastic or may misinterpret friendly gestures as threatening.

Challenges in forming and maintaining relationships: Building and maintaining friendships can be particularly difficult for individuals with autism. They may find it hard to understand social norms and expectations, leading to potential conflicts or misunderstandings. This difficulty can result in social isolation, as they may feel unsure about how to approach others or sustain conversations.

Limited interest in social interactions or difficulty initiating conversations: Many individuals with autism may prefer solitary activities over social engagements. They might find social situations overwhelming or uninteresting, leading to a lack of motivation to initiate conversations or participate in group activities. This preference for solitude can sometimes be misconstrued as aloofness, but it often stems from a desire for comfort and familiarity.

Understanding these social interaction challenges is crucial for encouraging supportive environments where individuals with autism can thrive and feel included.

Communication Difficulties:

Delayed speech and language skills: Some individuals with autism may experience significant delays in developing spoken language. While some may eventually learn to speak, others may remain non-verbal throughout their lives. This can impact their ability to communicate needs, thoughts, and feelings effectively, leading to frustration for both the individual and those trying to interact with them.

Preference for non-verbal communication (e.g., gestures, pictures): Many individuals with autism often rely on non-verbal forms of communication, such as gestures, pictures, or communication devices. This preference can stem from difficulties in verbal expression or comfort with alternative methods. For instance, they may use visual supports like picture exchange systems to convey their wants or needs, which can be essential for effective communication.

Echolalia (repeating words or phrases):
Echolalia refers to the repetition of words or phrases that an individual has heard, sometimes immediately after hearing them or after a delay. This can occur with or without understanding the meaning behind the words. While echolalia can serve as a means of communication, it may also reflect an attempt to process language or convey feelings. For example, a child might repeat a phrase from a favorite show when excited or anxious, using it as a way to express themselves.

Recognizing these communication difficulties is vital for effective interaction and support, particularly in environments such as law enforcement, where clear communication is essential. Understanding and adapting to these unique communication styles can lead to more positive outcomes in interactions with individuals on the autism spectrum.

Repetitive Behaviors and Restricted Interests:

Engaging in repetitive movements (e.g., hand-flapping, rocking): Many individuals with autism engage in repetitive movements, such as hand-flapping, rocking, spinning, or other actions. These behaviors often provide comfort and can serve as a coping mechanism to manage anxiety or sensory overload. For some, these movements are a way to self-soothe or maintain focus in overwhelming situations.

Strong attachment to specific routines or rituals: Individuals with autism often develop strong attachments to specific routines or rituals. These routines provide predictability and security in their daily lives. Changes to these established routines can be distressing and may lead to increased anxiety or behavioral challenges. For example, a simple alteration in the order of daily activities can cause significant upset, as individuals may feel unprepared or disoriented.

Intense focus on particular subjects or interests: Many individuals on the autism spectrum exhibit an intense focus on particular subjects or interests, sometimes referred to as "special interests." This can manifest as deep, specialized knowledge about topics such as trains, animals, or technology. While this focus can be a source of joy and expertise, it may also lead to challenges in social situations if the individual has difficulty shifting topics or engaging in broader conversations.

Sensory Sensitivities:

Over- or under-sensitivity to sensory input (e.g., sounds, lights, textures): Individuals with autism often experience over or under-sensitivity to various sensory stimuli, such as sounds, lights, textures, and smells. For some, certain noises may feel unbearably loud or irritating, while others might not register sounds that are noticeable to most people. Similarly, some individuals may find certain textures uncomfortable or distressing, while others may seek out intense sensory experiences, such as spinning or touching different surfaces.

Difficulty in environments with loud noises or bright lights: Crowded or noisy environments, such as shopping malls, concerts, or busy streets, can be particularly challenging for individuals with autism. The overwhelming amount of sensory input can lead to anxiety, confusion, or distress. In response, some individuals may withdraw, seek quiet spaces, or exhibit behaviors that indicate they are overwhelmed. It is important for caregivers and law enforcement to recognize these signs and provide support by creating calmer environments or allowing for breaks when needed.

A common behavior often associated with autism is covering one's ears. This reaction stems from a heightened sensitivity to sound, a sensory trait that many autistic individuals experience. For some, sounds that others might merely find irritating can be overwhelmingly intense or even physically painful.

To better understand this, consider the universally grating noise of nails scraping down a blackboard or the piercing squeal of microphone feedback. Most people find these sounds unpleasant, but for autistic individuals, similar auditory experiences might come from the everyday noises others barely notice. The hum of fluorescent lights, the constant chatter of a crowded room, or the high-pitched beeping of a timer can feel intrusive, as though the sounds are attacking their senses.

This hypersensitivity can lead to sensory overload, a state where the brain struggles to process the barrage of stimuli, resulting in discomfort, anxiety, or even physical pain. For many autistic people, covering their ears isn't just a reaction; it's a way to self-regulate and create a barrier against the overwhelming auditory environment.

Understanding and respecting sensory sensitivities is crucial, not only in recognizing the challenges autistic individuals face but also in building environments that minimize distressing sensory inputs. For first responders, this awareness is particularly important, as the tools and sounds we are associated with, such as vehicle sirens, the tone of our voice, the clacking of our keys, the noise of a passing car, or even the ticking sound of a turn signal, can all contribute to sensory overload for someone on the spectrum. In some cases, these seemingly minor noises can cause significant distress or even physical pain. I myself have personally chosen sometimes to not to use my car's turn signal in certain situations, knowing that the repetitive clicking sound can trigger my daughter and cause her discomfort, even physical pain. By being mindful of these challenges and accommodating sensory needs, caregivers, educators, and first responders can establish a more inclusive and supportive atmosphere. Simple adjustments, such as reducing noise levels or providing alternatives like noise-canceling headphones, can make an enormous difference in helping individuals with autism feel safer and more supported, especially during stressful situations.

Cognitive Profiles:

Variability in cognitive abilities, with some individuals showing average or above-average intelligence, while others may have intellectual disabilities: Autism encompasses a broad spectrum of cognitive profiles, reflecting significant variability in intellectual functioning among individuals. Some may exhibit average or above-average intelligence, demonstrating advanced skills in specific areas, such as math, art, or music. Others may experience intellectual disabilities, which can affect their learning and daily functioning.

This diversity in cognitive abilities means that the support needs of individuals on the autism spectrum can vary greatly. For example, those with higher cognitive abilities may require challenges that engage their interests and skills, while individuals with intellectual disabilities may benefit from more structured support and tailored educational strategies.

Recognizing and understanding these cognitive differences is essential for providing effective support and advocating the strengths of individuals with autism. Tailoring interventions and accommodations to meet each individual's unique cognitive profile can lead to more positive outcomes and greater overall success.

Understanding these characteristics is essential for effective communication and support, especially in law enforcement and other public service roles. By recognizing the unique social interactive challenges, communication difficulties, repetitive behaviors, restricted interests, sensory sensitivities, and cognitive profiles associated with autism, professionals can tailor their approaches to meet the needs of individuals on the spectrum.

In law enforcement, this understanding can lead to more compassionate and effective interactions, reducing the risk of misunderstandings and ensuring that individuals feel safe and respected. Training first responders to recognize these traits can help them respond appropriately during encounters, whether in routine situations or crisis scenarios.

By aiding an environment of empathy and awareness, law enforcement and public service professionals can play a crucial role in supporting individuals with autism, ultimately enhancing community relationships and promoting inclusivity.

Myths and Misconceptions

There are several myths and misconceptions surrounding autism that can lead to misunderstanding and stigma. It's important to know these myths but note they don't end here. There are many more out there that we are not discussing, as these are the most prevalent in Law Enforcement you may be faced with.

1. **Myth: Autism is caused by bad parenting.**

The Fact is, Autism is a complex neurodevelopmental disorder that arises from a combination of biological and genetic factors. Extensive research has shown that parenting styles do not cause autism. This misconception can lead to unnecessary guilt and stigma for parents, making it crucial to understand that autism is not the result of how a child is raised. Instead, it is a condition that involves various neurological differences. Promoting awareness of this fact is vital in creating a supportive environment for families affected by autism, having understanding rather than blame.

2. **Myth: All individuals with autism have the same abilities and challenges.**

It's important to remember that Autism is a spectrum disorder, which means that individuals can exhibit a wide range of experiences, abilities, and challenges. Each person with autism is unique, possessing their own strengths and difficulties. This variability can manifest in various ways, such as differences in communication styles, social skills, cognitive abilities, and sensory sensitivities. Because of this diversity, it is essential to tailor support and interventions to meet the specific needs of each individual. Recognizing and celebrating these differences can lead to more effective support strategies and promote a more inclusive environment.

3. **Myth: Individuals with autism lack empathy.**

While some individuals with autism may find it challenging to express or interpret emotions in typical ways, many possess a strong capacity for empathy. They may experience feelings deeply but might express them differently than neurotypical individuals. Understanding these differences in emotional expression can enhance communication and connection. By recognizing that individuals with autism can have rich emotional lives, we can encourage more supportive and empathetic interactions, ultimately promoting better understanding and relationships.

4. **Myth: Autism can be "cured."**

There is no cure for autism. It is a lifelong neurodevelopmental condition. However, early intervention and appropriate support can significantly enhance an individual's development, helping them acquire essential skills and lead fulfilling lives. The focus should be on understanding and supporting the unique needs of each individual, promoting their strengths and helping them navigate challenges. Emphasizing acceptance and support rather than a quest for a cure has a more inclusive and empowering environment for individuals with autism and their families.

5. **Myth: People with autism are all savants.**

While some individuals with autism may display extraordinary skills or talents, known as savant abilities, this is not representative of all individuals on the spectrum. Autism encompasses a wide range of abilities and challenges, and many individuals have diverse skill sets that do not conform to the savant stereotype.

Recognizing the broad spectrum of abilities allows for a more accurate understanding of autism and encourages support that focuses on each person's unique strengths and needs, rather than perpetuating narrow or misleading portrayals.

By debunking these myths, we can create a more informed and compassionate environment for individuals with autism, leading to better interactions and support across various settings, including law enforcement. This understanding not only promotes empathy but also reduces stigma, encouraging more inclusive communities. When society recognizes the diversity within the autism spectrum, it paves the way for tailored support and effective communication, ultimately enhancing the quality of life for individuals with autism and their families. Creating awareness and understanding is essential for building a society where everyone is valued and respected.

Understanding these definitions, characteristics, and myths is essential for empathy and facilitating effective interactions with individuals with autism, particularly in contexts like law enforcement or community support. By being informed, first responders and community members can respond more appropriately to the unique needs of individuals on the spectrum, reducing misunderstandings and promoting safety and respect. This knowledge helps build trust and rapport, allowing for better communication and support, ultimately leading to more positive outcomes for everyone involved.

De-escalation

Individuals with Autism Spectrum Disorder (ASD) often respond to stress in unique ways, and high-pressure situations can be particularly challenging for them. Training law enforcement first responders to recognize signs of distress and apply effective de-escalation techniques is crucial for ensuring safe, positive interactions. First responders who are prepared to handle these situations with care can reduce the likelihood of escalation and aid in trust with individuals on the spectrum.

One essential aspect of de-escalation is recognizing signs of distress. Individuals with autism may exhibit anxiety or overwhelm through specific behaviors, such as repetitive movements like hand-flapping or rocking. These repetitive behaviors often serve as self-soothing mechanisms during stressful moments. Avoidance or withdrawal, such as turning away, covering their ears, or attempting to leave, are also common coping strategies. Additionally, changes in vocalization, such as shifts in tone, volume, or the speed of speech, can signal that the individual is experiencing heightened stress.

Creating a calm environment is another critical component of de-escalation. First responders should strive to minimize environmental stressors by reducing background noise and speaking in a calm, quiet voice. Respecting the individual's personal space is equally important, as sudden movements or close physical proximity can increase anxiety. First responders should approach slowly and allow the person to feel comfortable without unnecessary pressure.

Using specific de-escalation techniques can further enhance communication and reduce tension. Simple, clear language helps avoid confusion and ensures the individual can understand instructions. Offering choices, such as deciding where to sit or how to proceed, empowers the person and helps prevent feelings of helplessness. Active listening and acknowledging the individual's feelings are also vital in establishing trust and reducing anxiety.

Whenever possible, first responders should involve supportive figures such as family members, caregivers, or advocates who can provide additional context and reassurance. These trusted individuals can help bridge communication gaps and offer insight into effective ways to engage with the person. By recognizing distress, creating a calm environment, and applying thoughtful de-escalation strategies, law enforcement first responders can ensure safer, more respectful interactions with individuals on the autism spectrum.

By mastering these de-escalation techniques, law enforcement first responders can create a more supportive environment, leading to safer outcomes for individuals with autism and the community at large.

Community Relations

Building trust between law enforcement and the communities they serve is essential for effective policing and public safety. Demonstrating understanding and sensitivity towards individuals with Autism Spectrum Disorder (ASD) plays a vital role in developing this relationship. First responders who actively engage with individuals on the spectrum and their families can create a more inclusive and supportive environment, leading to safer and more positive interactions.

Promoting understanding within the community is a key starting point. First responders who are knowledgeable about autism can help dispel myths and misconceptions, reducing stigma. Engaging in outreach initiatives, such as workshops or informational sessions, can raise awareness and empathy among community members. These efforts build bridges of understanding, encouraging the community to view first responders as allies and advocates for individuals with autism.

Building relationships with families and caregivers is another critical aspect of trust-building. Establishing connections and offering contact information opens lines of communication, ensuring families feel comfortable reaching out when needed. This support network can help first responders provide more effective assistance during encounters with individuals on the spectrum.

Participating in community events further strengthens relationships. First responders who attend autism awareness walks or family support gatherings demonstrate their commitment to understanding the unique needs of individuals with autism. Visibility at these events shows that law enforcement is invested in the well-being of the community, reinforcing trust and mutual respect.

Creating feedback mechanisms also enhances trust. Providing opportunities for community members to share their experiences with law enforcement, through surveys, focus groups, or public forums, ensures transparency and allows concerns to be addressed openly. This feedback loop fosters accountability and continuous improvement.

Collaboration with autism organizations can help law enforcement agencies stay informed about best practices and available resources. Partnering with advocacy groups not only provides first responders with additional training opportunities but also promotes joint initiatives that enhance community inclusivity. Through these collaborations, law enforcement can better understand the evolving needs of individuals with autism and ensure their practices reflect compassion and competence.

By prioritizing these efforts, law enforcement can foster a culture of respect and support for individuals with autism, ultimately leading to stronger community relations and improved public safety for all.

Legal and Ethical Considerations

Understanding the legal and ethical rights of individuals with disabilities, including those with Autism Spectrum Disorder (ASD), is essential for law enforcement first responders. Proper knowledge of these rights ensures first responders treat individuals with autism fairly, respecting both their legal protections and their dignity during interactions.

A key component is familiarity with disability rights laws. The Americans with Disabilities Act (ADA) prohibits discrimination against individuals with disabilities in public life, including interactions with law enforcement. First responders must ensure they provide fair treatment, avoiding actions that could constitute discrimination based on a person's condition. Additionally, the Individuals with Disabilities Education Act (IDEA), though primarily focused on education, emphasizes the need for accommodations, which can also apply to law enforcement scenarios, such as school-based interactions.

Reasonable accommodations are often necessary when engaging with individuals on the autism spectrum. First responders should be prepared to adapt their communication, such as using simple and direct language, allowing extra time for responses, or creating a calm environment to reduce anxiety. These adjustments help establish clearer interactions and reduce the likelihood of misunderstandings or escalation.

Informed consent is another important consideration, especially during searches, interrogations, or legal procedures. First responders must ensure individuals with autism understand the situation and their rights before proceeding, safeguarding ethical practices. Clear communication is essential in these moments to ensure that consent is both informed and valid.

Respect for confidentiality and privacy is paramount. First responders should handle sensitive information discreetly and avoid public discussions about an individual's condition or background. Conversations about personal matters should occur in private settings to maintain respect and trust.

Crisis intervention training specific to disabilities is critical for first responders to manage challenging situations. This specialized training equips law enforcement with the tools needed to de-escalate crises effectively while maintaining the dignity of all parties involved.

Finally, thorough documentation and reporting of interactions with individuals with autism ensure transparency and accountability. Detailed records provide a clear account of the encounter, supporting both the officer's actions and the individual's rights, while also contributing to improved practices in future interactions.

By being aware of these legal and ethical considerations, law enforcement first responders can better protect the rights and dignity of individuals with autism, nurturing trust and cooperation within the community. This understanding is key to ensuring equitable treatment and effective policing for all individuals, regardless of their abilities.

By prioritizing education and awareness of autism, first responders can significantly improve their response strategies, build community trust, and ensure more equitable treatment for individuals on the autism spectrum. This guide serves as a foundational resource for first responders seeking to enhance their understanding and skills in this critical area.

Key Takeaways

Increased Knowledge: Understanding autism's characteristics and challenges equips first responders to interact more effectively and compassionately with individuals on the spectrum.

Enhanced Communication: Adapting communication techniques can prevent misunderstandings and reduce conflict, creating a more supportive environment.

Effective De-escalation: Recognizing signs of distress and employing de-escalation techniques can lead to safer interactions for all parties involved.

Building Community Relations: Demonstrating sensitivity and understanding towards individuals with autism helps strengthen trust and rapport between law enforcement and the community.

Legal and Ethical Compliance: Knowledge of disability rights ensures that first responders uphold the law while respecting the dignity and rights of individuals with autism.

As the prevalence of autism continues to rise, first responders must be prepared to respond effectively and respectfully. Continuous training and a commitment to understanding autism will lead to more positive outcomes, enhancing public safety and community well-being. This guide is a starting point for first responders nationwide to build their competencies and create a more inclusive society for all.

Chapter 2

Understanding Autism Across the Lifespan

Raising a daughter with autism has been a journey filled with changes, challenges, and remarkable moments of growth. I vividly remember her first day of school. My wife put her on the bus, and the sheer look of terror on my daughter's face was heartbreaking, an expression that seemed to say we were giving her up. I am grateful I wasn't there in person and only saw it later through a video my wife recorded, as witnessing it firsthand would have been too difficult. Now, years later, she eagerly waits for the bus each morning, sometimes excited to leave even before it arrives.

In her early years, she would watch episode after episode of *Star Wars: The Clone Wars*, immersing herself in the adventures of the characters. This love for the show gradually evolved into a deep affection for *My Little Pony*, and eventually, *Disney* movies became a significant part of her world. Despite being non-verbal, her connection to these stories grew stronger, and she developed her own unique way of engaging with them, to drawing the characters, or mimicking their behaviors. One of the most remarkable things she does is sign *Walt*

Disney's name, just as it appears at the beginning of every *Disney* film. It's a beautiful expression of how much these films mean to her and how she's found a way to connect with the magic they offer.

As she has grown, her unique personality has truly blossomed. She has become quite the prankster, always delighting in pulling off jokes with a mischievous sparkle in her eyes. Her deep love for the ocean, especially sharks, has been another unexpected and fascinating development. At 11 years old, she could spend hours watching shark documentaries or playing *Assassin's Creed Odyssey*, where she swims in the game's virtual ocean just to be near the sharks.

    These experiences highlight an important truth for first responders: individuals with autism are just like anyone else; they have unique personalities, interests, and capabilities that change and adapt overtime. As a School Resource Officer I got to know and interact with an autistic boy who was deeply passionate about trains. He could list every locomotive engine and knew all the technical details, that quite frankly I did not care for, yet I listened with eager intent to learn, just so I could build a rapport with him. Over time, his focus shifted to airplanes, and he began to dream of becoming a pilot. Autism does not limit a person's ability to grow, evolve, and develop new interests; it simply means that their journey may take a different path, one that is often times held up by roadblocks not usually seen by others.

Even neurotypical children need time to develop their personalities and passions; why should it be any different for autistic individuals? This realization became especially poignant during a family cruise we took with an amazing company *Autism on the Seas* in March 2021. While leaving the beach one day, my daughter experienced a meltdown. Despite our best efforts to calm her and contain the situation, she found an opening between me and the staff and suddenly ran off. I gave chase, only to find her heading straight for the ocean. As she reached the water's edge, she paused, allowing the waves to gently wash over her feet, and I observed firsthand as her meltdown subsided, and was replaced by a visible calm.

Standing back, I watched as a sense of peace washed over her. The *Autism on the Seas* staff, who had been helping, stood quietly behind me, recognizing how the ocean grounded her. Moments later, my daughter knelt, kissed the water, and, in her own nonverbal way, said, "Love you." It was a powerful moment that showed me just how much the ocean completes her, filling her senses and bringing her joy.

Since then, we've adapted our approach when visiting the beach. We prepare her well in advance, coaching her on when we'll leave, and still we always allow her the time she needs to connect with the water before saying goodbye. These adjustments are small, but they make a significant difference in her experience.

For first responders, understanding and respecting these individual needs is essential. Autistic individuals are not defined by their diagnosis; they are unique, evolving people with deep feelings and incredible potential. Recognizing this is the first step toward building trust, understanding, and creating truly an inclusive community.

Autism in Children vs. Adults

Understanding autism requires an appreciation for how it manifests differently across various stages of life, particularly between children and adults. In children, autism often presents through sensory sensitivities and social challenges. These young individuals may react intensely to sensory stimuli such as loud noises or bright lights, and they may have difficulty understanding social cues, which can lead to misunderstandings or behavioral outbursts. In contrast, adults with autism might exhibit different traits, such as unique communication styles and struggles with independence. Adults may prefer clear, direct communication and might deal with challenges related to living independently, such as managing daily routines or social obligations.

As first responders encounter autistic individuals across these age groups, it is crucial for them to tailor their approaches to meet age-specific needs effectively. For children, employing simpler language and a gentle tone can help in communicating effectively, while being mindful of their sensory sensitivities by minimizing unnecessary noise or sudden movements. Conversely, when interacting with autistic adults, first responders can benefit from providing personal space to respect their potential need for boundaries and using a straightforward communication style to ensure clarity and comprehension. By adapting their methods based on the developmental stage and individual characteristics of autistic individuals, first responders not only enhance the quality of their interventions but also build trust and understanding in these critical interactions.

Supporting Aging Autistic Individuals

Supporting aging autistic individuals involves acknowledging and addressing the unique challenges they face as they grow older. As these individuals advance in age, they may experience cognitive changes similar to the broader aging population, yet these changes can be more pronounced in the context of autism. Increased health issues may arise, affecting both physical and mental well-being, and the likelihood of social isolation can also heighten, often due to a lack of understanding and support within their communities. Aging autistic individuals may also struggle with rigidity in routines and changes in daily life, making transitions particularly stressful.

To effectively support this demographic, law enforcement and first responders should consider adapting their engagement strategies to be more inclusive and sensitive to their needs. Training programs that focus on recognizing the signs of autism in adults can enhance the ability of officers to identify and appropriately interact with autistic individuals. Such training can include understanding common stressors and behaviors associated with autism, as well as learning de-escalation techniques tailored to address potential distress during interactions. This might involve using calm and reassuring communication, allowing extra time for responses, and minimizing physical contact unless necessary. By adopting these methods, law enforcement can not only improve the safety and outcome of their encounters with aging autistic individuals but also encourage a more supportive and empathetic community environment.

Key Strategies

We've talked a lot about communication but it's important to note when it comes to communicating with autistic individuals, first responders **must** employ tailored strategies that recognize the developmental and experiential differences between children and adults. Children on the autism spectrum often require communication that is straightforward and free from complex language or idiomatic expressions. They may rely heavily on non-verbal cues, such as gestures or visual aids, to process information effectively. Adults, on the other hand, may have developed personal communication styles over time, which could range from using literal language to having advanced vocabulary skills. However, they might still face challenges with abstract concepts or nuanced emotional expressions. Both age groups benefit significantly from the use of non-verbal communication elements, yet the execution may vary. With children, visual aids or familiar objects can provide comfort and understanding, while with adults, maintaining an open and approachable body language can facilitate clearer interactions.

Building trust and rapport with autistic individuals requires a keen sensitivity to their need for routine and predictability. For children, this might mean respecting their comfort zones, such as familiar toys or settings, and maintaining a consistent approach throughout interactions. Adults might prefer predictability in conversation topics or the sequence of events during an encounter. Abiding by these preferences helps reduce anxiety and increases a sense of security. First responders should take extra time to observe and recognize behavioral cues that indicate discomfort or distress, adapting their approach accordingly to avoid overwhelming the individual.

To support these strategies, ongoing training and education for first responders is essential. Training programs should focus on increasing autism awareness by incorporating both theoretical knowledge and practical skills, such as role-playing scenarios or simulations that replicate interactions with autistic individuals. Successful models include programs like CIT (Crisis Intervention Team) training, which emphasizes de-escalation techniques and mental health awareness, or community-based workshops where first responders can learn directly from autistic individuals and advocacy organizations about best practices and common challenges.

Community engagement plays a vital role in supporting autistic individuals and their families. By collaborating with autism organizations, first responders can gain valuable insights and resources to enhance their understanding and skills. Community involvement also helps build a supportive network that encourages social inclusion and advocacy for autistic individuals. With these partnerships, communities can create environments where autistic individuals feel safe, understood, and respected. This collaboration extends beyond the immediate need for emergency response, influencing broader social attitudes and helping to develop policies that support and empower autistic individuals and their families.

Chapter 3

Strategies for Effective Communication

Communicating with someone on the autism spectrum, especially in crisis situations, presents unique challenges and requires an understanding far beyond traditional methods. Whether the person is verbal or nonverbal, their responses can vary widely, and it's our job to adapt. As responders, we've all seen scenarios where a well-thought-out approach has made all the difference and, unfortunately, cases where things escalated unnecessarily, often due to a lack of patience or understanding. Too often, I've seen first responders jump directly to force or aggressive tactics, not out of malice, but out of a lack of awareness about autism and the nuances of communication it requires. While there are absolutely situations where force is necessary and appropriate, too many times it's used prematurely, resulting in outcomes that might have been avoided with a different approach.

I recall one specific call that has stayed with me. I responded to a report of a teenage girl with autism at a campground who had armed herself with a knife and was threatening her parents. When I arrived, I quickly got her parents to step out of the camper to create some space and minimize tension. I positioned myself between them and their daughter, assessing the situation carefully. The girl still held the knife, and I had no idea what might set her off. With my firearm drawn but held low, I carefully moved behind the kitchen island, using it as a buffer between us. At that moment, it was just the two of us in this high-stakes standoff, and all I had were my words and whatever rapport I could build to reach her.

For the next 20 to 30 minutes, I cycled through every approach I could think of, trying everything from direct communication to softer "verbal judo" tactics. Nothing seemed to break through. But then, somehow, I stumbled on an idea, I mentioned a Twix candy bar. Maybe I had seen a wrapper nearby, or maybe it was just a shot in the dark. But when I mentioned it, her eyes flickered with interest. That one word created a connection. I immediately ran with it, talking about candy, favorite snacks, and eventually, a calm rapport started to build. The Twix bar became a bridge that helped her feel safe enough to put down the knife, and we both stepped outside together to talk. By the time backup arrived, we were sitting at a picnic table, simply chatting, and the tension of those first few minutes had completely dissolved.

Years later, I would run into this girl on various calls. Often, she would greet me with a smile and a "You're the Twix officer," and I knew I had her trust. But one day, things were different. She was having a bad day, and when she saw me, her reaction was immediate and direct: "Fuck off, I don't want to talk to you." She turned to my partner, indicating she'd rather speak with her instead. In that moment, I knew that this wasn't personal; she simply needed a different approach, a different face, maybe a different style of communication. I respected that and stepped back, letting my partner take the lead. She connected with her, and the situation de-escalated smoothly. I understood that it wasn't about me or my ego; it was about knowing when to be the right person to step in and when to step back and allow someone else to help.

This experience highlighted to me the importance of flexibility in communication, especially with individuals on the spectrum. Building rapport in one situation doesn't guarantee that same approach will work in another. People change, circumstances change, and we as first responders need to adapt our communication styles to meet those needs. Learning to recognize those shifts and respond with openness, patience, and creativity is crucial in helping to prevent crises from escalating. In the end, it's about connecting as human beings, meeting people where they are in that moment, and understanding that true communication is as much about listening as it is about speaking. This adaptability has become one of the most valuable tools in my approach, allowing me to reach people in ways that standard tactics never could.

Verbal and Non-Verbal Techniques

Effective communication with individuals on the autism spectrum requires a blend of verbal and non-verbal strategies. By integrating these approaches, you can create a supportive environment that aids in understanding and connection.

Believe it or not, many studies have explored the intriguing idea of telepathy as a form of communication among nonverbal individuals with autism. One recent study delved into this phenomenon, observing hundreds of nonverbal autistic children in a carefully controlled setting. In the study, the children were placed in a separate room from their parents. The researchers would show the parents an object, color, or number on a screen, and then observe how the nonverbal child would communicate the same information through their chosen communication device. Remarkably, the children identified the correct object, color, or number with an astonishing 95% accuracy.

This raises fascinating questions about the depth of connection and intuitive understanding that can exist between individuals on the spectrum and those who are closest to them. While the mechanisms behind such phenomena are still being studied, the implications for first responders are profound. Recognizing that communication is not limited to words or even traditional methods is essential when interacting with individuals on the autism spectrum.

For first responders, this means not only adapting their approach to engage with the individual directly but also understanding the critical role parents or caregivers play in facilitating communication. A parent's insight into their child's unique behaviors, preferences, and nonverbal cues can provide a roadmap for building trust and ensuring a successful interaction. Ignoring or undervaluing this connection could lead to misunderstandings, while embracing it could be the key to de-escalating a potentially stressful situation.

By staying open-minded and informed about emerging studies and alternative forms of communication, first responders can better equip themselves to connect with individuals on the spectrum in meaningful and effective ways. This understanding could be the difference between a positive, respectful interaction and unintentionally creating fear or frustration. First responders should always try to abide by each of the following, when communicating with someone on the spectrum.

Calm tone: Using a soft, soothing voice is crucial in reducing anxiety during interactions. A gentle tone can create a sense of safety and reassurance, making the individual feel more comfortable. This approach helps establish a positive environment for communication, encouraging openness and understanding.

Clear Speech: Speak clearly and at a moderate pace to enhance understanding. Avoid using slang, idioms, or complex phrases, as these can lead to confusion. Strive for straightforward language that is easy to follow, ensuring your message is communicated effectively. This clarity helps build trust and facilitates better interaction.

Use of Visual Aids: Incorporating visual aids, such as pictures, diagrams, or written instructions—can significantly enhance understanding. These tools provide a concrete reference that complements verbal communication, making concepts easier to grasp. Visuals can clarify instructions, reduce anxiety, and help individuals process information more effectively, leading to improved interactions.

Body Language: Maintain open and non-threatening body language to demonstrate a sense of safety. Avoid crossing your arms or standing too close, as these gestures can be perceived as aggressive. Instead, keep an open posture and respect personal space. This approach helps create a more comfortable environment, encouraging positive communication and interaction.

Active Listening: Demonstrate engagement through active listening by nodding and maintaining appropriate eye contact. These behaviors signal attentiveness and respect, showing the individual that you are fully present in the conversation. Active listening helps build rapport, making it easier for the person to express themselves and feel understood.

Using Simple Language

Simplifying language is essential when communicating with individuals on the autism spectrum. Clear and direct language minimizes confusion and enhances understanding. By using straightforward vocabulary and avoiding complex phrases, you create a more accessible communication environment, allowing for more effective interactions.

Short Sentences: Use concise and straightforward sentences to communicate effectively. Lengthy explanations can overwhelm the listener, making it harder for them to process information. By keeping your statements brief and clear, you promote better understanding and facilitate a smoother conversation.

Direct Questions: Ask clear and direct questions that invite simple yes or no answers. This approach simplifies communication and reduces ambiguity. For example, instead of asking, "What would you like to do next?" you might say, "Do you want to sit down?" This helps the individual focus on a specific choice, making it easier for them to respond.

Avoid Ambiguity: Be specific in your language to prevent confusion. Instead of using vague phrases like, "Let's go over there," specify the location clearly, such as, "Let's go to the blue chair." This clarity helps the individual understand exactly what you mean, making it easier for them to follow instructions and engage in the conversation.

Repeat and Rephrase: If confusion arises, take the time to repeat or rephrase your question or instruction. This can help clarify your message and facilitate understanding. For example, if the individual seems unsure, you might say, "Let me say that again: Do you want to sit down in the blue chair?" This approach reinforces your communication and ensures the individual feels supported in processing the information.

Using simple language with individuals with autism is crucial for effective communication and understanding. Clear and straightforward language minimizes confusion and helps individuals process information more easily, reducing the likelihood of frustration and anxiety. Many individuals on the spectrum may take longer to grasp complex concepts, so using concise vocabulary and direct questions allows them to engage more comfortably in conversations. This approach not only clarifies expectations but also encourages active participation, empowering individuals to respond with confidence. Ultimately, simplifying language creates a supportive environment that enhances interactions and builds trust, making communication more accessible and effective.

Establishing Trust and Rapport

Building trust and rapport is essential for effective communication with individuals on the autism spectrum. Establishing a positive relationship creates a safe environment where individuals feel comfortable expressing themselves. Trust furthers openness, making it easier for them to engage in conversations and share their thoughts or feelings. By introducing yourself clearly and showing patience, you demonstrate respect for their unique communication styles. Additionally, being consistent in your interactions reinforces reliability, which further strengthens trust. When individuals feel understood and valued, they are more likely to participate actively, leading to more meaningful and effective communication. Overall, prioritizing trust and rapport lays the foundation for successful interactions and deeper connections.

Introduce Yourself: Starting interactions by clearly stating your name and role is vital in building trust and creating a sense of safety. This introduction establishes transparency, helping individuals on the autism spectrum understand who they are communicating with and what to expect. By providing this information upfront, you reduce uncertainty and anxiety, making the individual feel more comfortable. A clear introduction also signals respect and willingness to engage, fostering a more positive atmosphere for communication. Overall, this simple yet effective approach lays the groundwork for a supportive interaction.

Be Patient: Allowing extra time for responses is essential when communicating with individuals on the autism spectrum. Many may require additional time to process information and formulate their replies, so patience is key. Rushing or interrupting can lead to anxiety and hinder effective communication. By giving them the time they need, you demonstrate respect for their processing style and create a supportive environment. This approach not only fosters a sense of understanding but also encourages more meaningful and thoughtful exchanges, ultimately enhancing the quality of interaction.

Show Empathy: Acknowledging the individual's feelings and experiences is crucial for effective communication. Using empathetic phrases like, "I understand this is difficult," conveys that you are aware of their emotions and challenges. This recognition helps to validate their feelings, reassuring a sense of understanding and connection. Demonstrating empathy creates a supportive atmosphere where individuals feel heard and respected, making them more likely to engage openly in the conversation. Overall, showing empathy strengthens trust and rapport, enhancing the overall interaction experience.

Consistency: Consistency in communication and approach is vital for building trust with individuals on the autism spectrum. When your interactions are reliable and predictable, it fosters a sense of safety and security. If you promise to follow up or provide information, it's essential to follow through, as this reinforces your commitment and reliability. Consistent behavior helps individuals feel more comfortable and understood, making it easier for them to engage in conversations. By creating a stable environment through consistent communication, you enhance trust and facilitate more effective interactions.

Involve Caregivers: Involving caregivers or family members in the conversation is crucial when communicating with individuals on the autism spectrum. Caregivers can provide valuable context about the individual's preferences, communication style, and needs, improving the quality of engagement. Including them not only supports the individual but also supports a collaborative environment where everyone feels engaged. This approach can help clarify information and ensure that the individual receives the support they need, making communication more effective and meaningful. By recognizing the importance of caregivers, you strengthen the support network and promote a more inclusive conversation.

Understanding Stimming and self-calming behaviors

Stimming, or self-stimulatory behavior, is a common form of communication and regulation used by many autistic individuals. For first responders, understanding stimming is vital because it serves as a way for autistic people to manage sensory input, express emotions, and cope with stress. Stimming can manifest in a wide range of repetitive actions, such as hand flapping, light gazing, humming, tapping, rocking, or squeezing objects. These behaviors can be categorized into various types, including visual, auditory, tactile, vestibular, and proprioceptive. While some stimming behaviors may appear similar among individuals, no two autistic people are exactly alike. The ways individuals stim are uniquely personal and reflect their sensory preferences, emotional state, and coping mechanisms. For example, one person may flap their hands when excited, while another might hum to self-soothe when anxious. This variation means that stimming is not only diverse but also deeply tied to each person's unique experience of the world.

Understanding that stimming is a **natural response to stress or anxiety** is also key. Think about a time when you felt nervous or overwhelmed. You might have clicked a pen repeatedly, tapped your foot, bit your lip, or cracked your knuckles. That's stimming, though it might be less noticeable, it's still a self-soothing mechanism. Autistic individuals often use stimming to manage heightened emotions, sensory overload, or distress, providing them with a way to regulate their feelings and feel more in control. While it can look different, the underlying purpose of stimming is much the same for everyone: it's a tool for calming oneself.

For first responders, recognizing stimming behaviors is essential, as it can help identify someone who may be on the autism spectrum. You might observe hand flapping, rocking back and forth, light gazing, humming, repeating phrases, tapping on objects, rubbing surfaces, or even jumping or spinning. It's important to note that **stimming is not harmful in itself**, it's a natural, often necessary, response. Intervening without understanding the purpose of the behavior can lead to heightened anxiety or confusion for the individual. Instead, it's essential to **allow the person to continue stimming as long as it doesn't pose a risk to their safety or the safety of others**. This understanding can help prevent unnecessary escalation of the situation.

As you approach an autistic individual, you may notice their stimming behaviors intensify, which could signal increased anxiety or discomfort. This is often due to the unpredictability of the situation or the presence of unfamiliar people. In such cases, **giving space is crucial**. Step back and create a physical distance to allow the individual some breathing room. This can reduce immediate stress and help the person feel more at ease. Clear and calm communication is key. Explain your actions by using simple direct language. Instead of saying, "I need you to calm down," try saying, "I'm going to stand here while we talk," or "I'm going to help you with this." Autistic individuals may need extra time to process the situation, so **patience is essential**. Avoid rushing or making sudden movements, as this could increase their stress.

Ensuring the **safety of the individual and those around them** is always a priority. If the stimming behavior is not harmful, it's best to let it continue. It's a natural part of the individual's coping strategy and can provide comfort during times of anxiety. By recognizing and respecting stimming behaviors, first responders can better **build trust** with autistic individuals. This understanding creates opportunities to de-escalate situations with empathy and clarity, reducing the risk of misinterpretation or escalation. When stimming is allowed to occur in a safe and supportive environment, and when clear communication is maintained, first responders can provide more effective and compassionate care to autistic individuals.

Understanding Interests for Effective Search and Rescue:

Effective communication is crucial for first responders when it comes to locating missing individuals, particularly those on the autism spectrum. Recognizing and addressing the interests of autistic individuals can significantly impact the success of search and rescue operations. Understanding these interests is essential because it provides key insights that can guide search efforts more effectively.

For instance, statistics show that many individuals with autism have a strong attraction to bodies of water. In cases of missing autistic children aged 14 and younger, drowning accounts for 90% of fatalities. This statistic underscores a critical strategy for first responders: focusing initial search efforts on nearby water sources. By doing so, the likelihood of a successful recovery increases dramatically.

However, while water remains a primary area of focus, it's also important for first responders to gather information about the child's specific interests as the search progresses. These interests might include a fascination with airplanes, trains, or cars, which can guide the direction of the search. If a child is known to be intrigued by airplanes, for example, the search could be expanded to include nearby airports.

Additionally, understanding the multisensory appeal of water and why it attracts individuals with autism is vital. The calming effect that the sound, movement, taste and even scent of water can have on the sensory experiences of autistic children helps explain their tendency to gravitate towards it. This insight reinforces the significance of prioritizing water searches.

By using communication that accurately identifies the interests and environmental factors captivating to autistic children, first responders can enhance their strategies, potentially saving lives and improving the outcomes of their missions.

Understanding communication isn't always verbal or obvious

Communication for autistic individuals exists on many levels, and it's crucial for first responders to understand and adapt to these diverse forms of expression. While some autistic individuals may communicate verbally, many rely on nonverbal methods, such as tattoos, drawings, pictures, or even paintings. Consider tattoos for a moment. Each one is typically a form of personal storytelling or expressed interests in individuals. Many first responders have their own tattoos, each typically holds a significant meaning, representing a memory, or something special. Similar for autistic individuals and their families, tattoos can also serve as powerful symbols of communication and connection. Many autistic people who are Level 1 or Level 2 choose unique autism-related tattoos to express their identity or journey. Likewise, it's common for parents of autistic children to bear tattoos representing their love and dedication. I have a personal autism tattoo for my daughter, a permanent reminder of her and the bond we share, no matter where I go or what I do. It's also important to look for tattoos on both the individual and their parents, as they may provide valuable insight into the situation or the individual's needs.

When thinking about communication, it's essential to recognize that it evolves over time. Autistic individuals may transition from one form of communication to another as they grow and develop. For example, my daughter began communicating through sign language at a young age. While she still occasionally uses it, it's not as prevalent now as it once was. Over the years, she has progressed to using PECS (Picture Exchange Communication System) cards, talking tablets, and verbal cues. Each stage of this journey has been unique, and her forms of communication have reflected her personal growth.

One particularly meaningful example of my daughter's communication came through her artwork. When she was five, she painted four canvases, each representing a different season, winter, spring, summer, and fall. At first glance, they seemed to simply depict the seasons, but we noticed something unique about one painting. The brush strokes on the fall canvas were angled, unlike the up-and-down strokes on the others. This small detail revealed something profound: fall was her favorite season. Without her art, we might never have known this about her.

This story highlights a key point: communication isn't always verbal, and often, you need to "listen with your eyes." Observing the details in someone's expression, whether through their art, actions, or other nonverbal cues, can unlock critical insights. For first responders, this understanding is invaluable. Recognizing that communication can come in many forms, beyond words, is essential for effectively supporting autistic individuals. By being observant, patient, and open to these varied expressions, you can build trust and create a bridge to understanding in situations that might otherwise feel overwhelming or unclear.

Communicating through creativity:

Recently, our daughter has become captivated by Disney's *Inside Out 2*. She loves the movie on many levels, connecting with it in her own unique way. What's particularly special is how she's used the characters to help express her emotions to us. For her, Joy, Sadness, Anger, Fear, Disgust, Embarrassment, Envy, Ennui and Anxiety have become more than just characters, they're tools for communication.

One character stands out as her favorite: Anxiety. It seems to resonate with her deeply, and she often gravitates toward this character when choosing a way to express herself. Perhaps it's because Anxiety mirrors some of the challenges she experiences daily, the uncertainty, the heightened sensitivity to her surroundings, and the overwhelming emotions that sometimes come with trying to navigate the world. Watching the movie, it's almost as if she sees herself reflected in the character, providing a sense of validation and understanding.

Inspired by this, we decided to update some of her PECS (Picture Exchange Communication System) cards to feature images of these emotions, including

Anxiety. Now, instead of struggling to articulate how she feels, she can point to a picture of the character that matches her mood. For example, if she's feeling anxious or unsettled, she'll show us Anxiety. If she's happy, she'll choose Joy; if upset, she might pick Anger or Sadness.

This small adjustment has been transformative for our family. It's given my wife and me a clearer window into her world, allowing us to better understand what she's experiencing and how she feels about it. By using a medium she's deeply connected to, we've created a more effective way to communicate and support her. It's a powerful reminder that sometimes, the best tools for connection are the ones that resonate most with the individual.

Conclusion

By implementing all these strategies, first responders can significantly enhance their communication skills, creating a more supportive environment for individuals with autism. This understanding makes for more effective interactions, reducing the potential for misunderstandings, and ensuring that individuals feel heard and respected. As a result, stronger community relationships can develop, promoting trust and collaboration between first responders and the autism community. By prioritizing these communication techniques, first responders not only improve the quality of their interactions but also contribute to a more inclusive and understanding society.

  When trying to communicate with someone on the spectrum and it seems like all efforts are failing, don't underestimate the power of simplicity. When all else fails, use your pen and paper. Every first responder carries these tools, and they can become invaluable in bridging the communication gap. Start by writing the word "Name", followed by a colon, and then draw a line. Think about it: many autistic children go to school, and a familiar task for them is writing their name at the top of a paper. This small, straightforward action can establish a connection through something they recognize and understand. By showing them something familiar, you create an anchor in what might feel like an overwhelming situation, helping them respond in a way that feels safe and approachable. This approach, paired with patience and observation, can be a game-changer in creating meaningful and effective communication.

Chapter 4

Approach Techniques

When approaching any scene, as officers we automatically start playing the "what if" game. It's something that happens whether we want it to or not. What if things go smoothly? What if they don't? What if they try to run, or they pull a weapon? And yes, at times, there's even the haunting question: *What if I don't make it home after this call?* These thoughts are always in the back of our minds, running through scenarios even when we're not consciously focused on them. And while this mindset may seem intense, it's actually a key part of staying prepared, allowing us to adapt quickly and make informed choices as situations evolve.

One call in particular stands out to me as a reminder of why playing the "what if" game can be crucial. I was training a new officer at the time when we were dispatched to respond to a young autistic boy who had run away from home following an argument with his mother. He hadn't committed any crime, he just wanted to get away, to escape whatever tension had built up at home. As we arrived, another officer had already located him walking along the side of the road, so we joined in, hoping to safely guide him back without escalating the situation.

At first, he didn't respond to us, keeping his distance and walking further away. He wasn't causing harm, but he was edging closer to traffic, and as he turned off the road and started into a nearby field, we followed to make sure he stayed safe. I sent my rookie and another officer to keep up with him on foot, while I made my way back to the roadway where our vehicles were parked. I didn't know it at the time, but this decision was about to make a huge difference.

As soon as I got back to the road, I saw him bolting from the field, sprinting straight toward our vehicles. Thankfully, I had my keys in hand and made sure my vehicle was locked, assuming the other officer had done the same. But then, I saw the door open and my heart dropped. Without hesitating, I sprinted across the road, paying no attention to traffic, knowing I had to get there before he could lock himself inside and possibly take control of the vehicle. I made it just in time, opening the door and jumping practically on top of him in the drivers seat. He was already reaching for the gear shift, and I held it firmly in park, bracing myself as he fought back.

    The struggle was intense, his adrenaline was high, and he was determined to take control. I drew my taser from its holster aiming it towards his chest and threatening to tase him. Within moments, my rookie and the other officer arrived, and together we managed to safely remove him from the vehicle and place him in handcuffs to prevent any further escalation.

    Looking back, the approach we took initially had been the best one at that time. We were careful not to intimidate him or make him feel trapped. He hadn't committed a crime, and our primary goal was simply to keep him safe. But then, in the blink of an eye, everything shifted. He ran, and the "what ifs" turned into reality. What if he got into the car and drove away? What if he accidentally hurt himself, or worse? In those moments, there wasn't time to hesitate or second-guess.

In this profession, situations can change in an instant, and that "what if" mindset prepares us to make split-second decisions that can save lives. This call taught me the value of adaptability and quick thinking, of staying one step ahead not just for my own safety but for the safety of the individuals I'm trying to protect. For this young boy, it was an innocent yet impulsive moment that could have ended very differently had we not reacted in time. These experiences stay with us, reminding us that every call is unique, every individual different, and that our role requires a constant readiness to adapt, to adjust, and to do whatever it takes to keep everyone safe.

Creating a calm environment is essential in any situation, but it is especially crucial when interacting with individuals on the autism spectrum. A calm setting can significantly reduce stress, enhance communication, and promote positive outcomes during interactions. There are several key reasons why maintaining a peaceful atmosphere is so important when working with autistic individuals.

Power of a Calm Space

First, a calm environment helps reduce anxiety. Sensory overload, such as loud noises, bright lights, and cluttered visuals, can cause heightened stress for individuals with autism. By minimizing these stimuli, individuals feel more secure and less overwhelmed, leading to a more stable interaction. Additionally, a tranquil environment enhances communication. When distractions are reduced, individuals can focus better on conversations, allowing for clearer and more effective exchanges.

Creating a peaceful setting also promotes comfort and safety. When individuals feel at ease in their surroundings, they are more likely to engage positively and express themselves openly. This sense of comfort also supports emotional regulation, helping individuals process their feelings in a controlled manner and reducing the likelihood of emotional distress or meltdowns.

Moreover, a calm environment encourages positive interactions. When individuals feel secure, they are more open to social engagement, which fosters stronger relationships with peers, caregivers, and professionals. This, in turn, enhances their sense of belonging. A peaceful space also facilitates learning and development, as it allows individuals to focus and absorb information without unnecessary distractions, supporting cognitive growth.

Lastly, a calm and predictable environment increases independence. By providing a stable setting, individuals can develop coping strategies and self-regulation skills, empowering them to navigate challenging situations with greater autonomy. In these ways, creating a calm environment not only supports individuals with autism but also enables more meaningful and productive interactions for everyone involved.

Establishing a calm environment is essential for enhancing the overall well-being of individuals on the autism spectrum, enabling them to thrive in social, educational, and personal contexts. Some ways you can help enhance the overall situation are: **Minimize Noise and Distractions, Maintain a Comfortable Distance, Use Soft Lighting, and Limit Visual Clutter.**

Minimize Noise and Distractions: When interacting with individuals on the autism spectrum, it's essential to find a quieter space. Move away from loud noises, flashing lights, and large crowds whenever possible. This not only helps create a more comfortable environment but also significantly reduces anxiety, allowing for clearer communication and a more positive interaction. Aim for settings that are calm and serene, where the individual can feel safe and at ease.

Maintain a Comfortable Distance: It's important to be mindful of personal space when interacting with individuals on the autism spectrum. Standing too close can feel intimidating and overwhelming. Aim for a distance that allows the individual to feel safe and secure. This not only inspires a sense of comfort but also encourages open communication. Pay attention to their body language; if they seem tense or uncomfortable, adjust your distance accordingly to help them feel more at ease.

Use Soft Lighting: When indoors, consider using softer, less harsh lighting to create a calming environment. Bright lights can be overwhelming and may increase anxiety for some individuals. Opt for lamps with warm light bulbs or dimmers to create a more soothing atmosphere. This gentle lighting can help individuals feel more relaxed and secure, facilitating better communication and interaction. Consider turning off your overhead lights if the situation permits. Often times these lights can cause the individual to go into a fight or flight mode, which will cause further issues for you.

Limit Visual Clutter: Opt for environments that are less cluttered to help individuals on the autism spectrum focus better during interactions. A setting with fewer visual stimuli allows them to direct their attention to the conversation without becoming overwhelmed. By eliminating unnecessary distractions, you create a space where they can engage more fully, process information more effectively, and feel more comfortable expressing themselves. This thoughtful approach can significantly enhance communication and overall interactive quality.

Non-Threatening Body Language

Non-verbal cues are particularly important in communicating with individuals on the autism spectrum, as they can often rely more on these signals than on verbal language. Here are some key aspects to consider:

Open Posture

Body Language: Maintaining an open posture is essential when interacting with individuals on the autism spectrum. An effective way to convey openness begins with keeping your arms uncrossed. By keeping your arms relaxed and at your sides instead of crossing them, you signal that you are approachable and friendly, which helps reduce feelings of intimidation.

Additionally, it is important to ensure your shoulders are relaxed. Tension in your shoulders can be perceived as defensive or anxious, potentially increasing discomfort for the individual you are engaging with. A relaxed posture can create a more inviting environment.

Another key aspect is to face the individual directly. Positioning your body towards the person you are communicating with demonstrates that you are engaged and attentive, having a sense of connection and trust. Furthermore, leaning slightly forward can indicate interest and attentiveness, encouraging the individual to engage more comfortably in the conversation.

By adopting an open posture, you create a welcoming atmosphere that encourages trust and positive interaction. This approach makes it easier for individuals on the autism spectrum to communicate and express themselves, ultimately enhancing the quality of your interaction.

Facial Expressions

Convey Warmth: Your facial expressions play a vital role in communication, especially when interacting with individuals on the spectrum. A few key points can enhance this aspect of your engagement.

First and foremost, a warm smile is essential. A gentle, genuine smile can establish trust and convey friendliness and approachability, making the individual feel more at ease in the interaction. Alongside your smile, ensure that you use soft eyes. Relaxed, kind eye expressions can show comfort, while intense or penetrating gazes may be perceived as threatening.

In addition to these expressions, it's beneficial to nod and react appropriately. Subtle nods or responsive facial cues, such as raising your eyebrows in understanding, can reinforce that you are engaged and attentive during the conversation. Conversely, it's important to avoid negative expressions. Be mindful of any facial cues that might communicate frustration or impatience. Maintaining a calm and pleasant demeanor encourages a more positive interaction.

By employing friendly and gentle facial expressions, you create a comforting environment that helps individuals on the autism spectrum feel safe and supported. This approach facilitates better communication and connection, ultimately enhancing the overall interaction.

Slow Movements

Deliberate Actions: Moving calmly and deliberately is crucial when interacting with individuals on the autism spectrum. Implementing this approach effectively can significantly enhance communication and comfort during your interactions.

One essential aspect is to use controlled gestures. Slow, purposeful movements help prevent startling the individual and allow them to process your actions more comfortably. This can be particularly important in high-stress situations where abrupt movements may cause anxiety.

When it comes to approaching individuals, doing so gradually is vital. For instance, if you need to hand something to them, extend your arm slowly to give them time to adjust to your presence. This gradual approach helps create a sense of security and control for the individual.

In addition, practicing mindful transitions is beneficial. Whether you are shifting your body position or changing your focus, doing so in a measured way can provide reassurance and predictability in the interaction. Consistency in your movements increases a more comfortable atmosphere.

Lastly, ensure that your facial expressions align with your slow movements. For example, if you're smiling while moving slowly, it reinforces a sense of calm and safety, making it easier for the individual to engage with you.

By being mindful of your movements and keeping them slow and deliberate, you create a more comfortable environment that furthers trust and open communication with individuals on the autism spectrum. This thoughtful approach can lead to more positive and meaningful interactions.

Kneeling or Sitting at Eye Level

Reduce Intimidation: Meeting individuals on the spectrum at their eye level can significantly enhance the comfort and effectiveness of your interactions. This approach can create a more welcoming environment and better communication.

To begin, consider kneeling or sitting down if the situation allows. By matching their height, you help reduce the physical power dynamic, making the interaction feel more personal and less threatening.

This simple adjustment can make a world of difference in how the individual perceives the interaction.

Establishing comfort is crucial. Positioning yourself at eye level can help individuals feel more secure and respected, encouraging them to engage more openly in the conversation. When individuals feel respected, they are more likely to respond positively.

Additionally, be mindful of space when transitioning to this position. Ensure that your movements are slow and deliberate, demonstrating consideration for their comfort. This mindfulness helps individuals adjust to your presence and can ease any anxiety they may feel.

While at their level, it is important to maintain gentle eye contact. This conveys attentiveness and warmth, further encouraging trust and encouraging effective communication.

By kneeling or sitting at eye level, you create a more approachable atmosphere that helps individuals on the autism spectrum feel safe and understood. This thoughtful approach facilitates better interactions, ultimately leading to more positive outcomes.

Gestures and Signaling

Use Simple Gestures: Incorporating gentle, clear gestures into your communication can significantly enhance understanding, particularly when interacting with individuals on the autism spectrum. Implementing effective strategies in this area can make your interactions more accessible and engaging.

One key strategy is to utilize clear hand signals. Straightforward hand gestures can complement your words and help convey meaning. For example, a thumbs-up can indicate approval, while an open hand can signal a welcome. These simple gestures can create clarity in communication and provide visual cues for understanding.

Additionally, consider using demonstrative actions when explaining something. For instance, if you are discussing an action like sitting down, mimic the movement to visually reinforce your message. This not only aids comprehension but also engages the individual in the conversation.

It's important to avoid overly complex gestures. Keeping gestures simple and consistent helps prevent confusion or overwhelm. Rapid or intricate movements can be difficult for individuals to interpret, so aim for clarity and straightforwardness in your gestures.

Furthermore, pairing gestures with verbal cues can enhance your communication. This multisensory approach allows individuals to grasp what you are conveying more effectively. Combining visual and auditory information can reinforce your message and make it more memorable.

Finally, be mindful of reactions. Pay attention to how the individual responds to your gestures, adjusting your approach based on their comfort and understanding. This might mean using more or fewer gestures as needed to facilitate better communication.

By using simple, clear gestures and being mindful of non-verbal cues, you can significantly enhance communication with individuals on the spectrum. Adapting your body language makes interactions more thoughtful, accessible, engaging, and positive, helping to create a supportive environment. This approach can lead to: **Improved Understanding, Increased Trust, and Higher Interaction Quality**

Improved Understanding: Clear non-verbal signals help bridge communication gaps, making it easier for individuals to grasp your intentions and feelings.

Increased Trust: A welcoming demeanor and respectful body language create a sense of safety, encouraging individuals to engage and express themselves more openly.

Higher Interaction Quality: By creating an atmosphere that prioritizes comfort and clarity, interactions become more meaningful and effective, promoting positive relationships.

Techniques for De-escalation

De-escalation techniques are essential for managing situations that may become tense or overwhelming, especially when interacting with individuals on the autism spectrum. Here are some effective strategies:

Stay Calm

Composed Demeanor: Maintaining a calm presence is crucial when interacting with individuals on the autism spectrum. A composed demeanor not only helps the individual feel more at ease but also sets the tone for a more positive interaction. Here are some effective strategies to achieve this:

First, consider taking deep breaths. Slow, deep breathing can help you manage your own stress levels, creating a more serene environment for the individual. When you are calm, it naturally influences the atmosphere around you, allowing the other person to feel more secure.

Next, focus on using a steady voice. Speaking in a calm and even tone conveys reassurance, which can be particularly soothing for individuals with autism. This approach helps establish a sense of security, encouraging them to engage more openly in the conversation.

Additionally, pay attention to your controlled body language. Avoid tense or abrupt movements, and instead, keep your posture relaxed and open. This signals to the individual that you are approachable and not a threat, further promoting a safe environment for communication.

Finally, practice mindful reactions. Be aware of your emotional responses and strive to stay composed, even in challenging situations. Your ability to maintain calmness sets a positive example and encourages the individual to mirror that demeanor, resulting in a more productive interaction.

By embodying a composed demeanor, you create a sense of safety and trust, making it easier for individuals on the spectrum to engage and communicate effectively. This approach not only benefits the individual but also leads to more successful and meaningful exchanges.

Validate Feelings

Acknowledge Emotions: Recognizing and validating an individual's feelings is essential for effective communication. By taking the time to acknowledge their emotions, you can create a more supportive environment that furthers trust and understanding.

One way to do this is by using empathetic language. Phrases such as "I see that you are upset" or "It's okay to feel this way" demonstrate that you acknowledge their emotions. This validation can help the individual feel understood and valued.

It's also important to avoid dismissing feelings. Statements like "It's not a big deal" can minimize their emotions and make them feel unheard. Instead, express that their feelings are valid and significant. This acknowledgment can make a substantial difference in how they perceive the interaction.

Additionally, consider reflecting emotions. Paraphrasing or reflecting what they express, such as saying, "It sounds like you're feeling frustrated," encourages them to share more about their feelings. This approach helps deepen the conversation and can lead to better understanding.

Finally, maintain a supportive tone. Using a gentle and soothing voice can significantly influence how the individual perceives your acknowledgment of their feelings. Your tone should convey compassion and patience, further reinforcing the message that their emotions are valid.

By validating feelings, you help individuals feel heard and understood, which instils trust and promotes a more constructive interaction. This empathetic approach encourages open communication and can significantly reduce anxiety during challenging moments, ultimately leading to a more positive experience for everyone involved.

Offer Choices

Empower Individuals: Providing simple options is an effective way to help individuals on the autism spectrum feel more in control of their situation.

One effective approach is to present clear options. Offering two or three straightforward choices can help individuals make decisions without feeling overwhelmed. For instance, you might ask, "Would you like to sit down or take a walk?" This clarity allows them to feel more secure in their decision-making process.

In addition to verbal options, you can use visual aids. Incorporating pictures or symbols to illustrate the choices enhances understanding and makes the options more tangible. Visual aids can bridge communication gaps and provide additional support for individuals who may struggle with processing verbal information.

It's also important to encourage participation. Allowing individuals to express their preferences not only empowers them but also shows a sense of autonomy and involvement in the situation. This participation can enhance their engagement and comfort during interactions.

Furthermore, reassuring and supporting individuals after presenting options is crucial. Let them know that either choice is acceptable, which can help alleviate anxiety about making the "right" decision. This reassurance creates a more relaxed atmosphere and encourages open communication.

By offering choices, you empower individuals to take an active role in their interactions, significantly reducing feelings of helplessness and promoting a sense of agency. For example, if you want them to sit on the curb but don't mind where they choose to sit, letting them decide can lead to compliance. Ultimately, you achieve your goal while allowing them to feel as though they have made a choice, a more positive experience for everyone involved.

Use Redirecting Techniques

Gentle Redirection: Redirecting an individual's focus can be an effective strategy for helping them regain calm when they seem overwhelmed. Implementing gentle redirection can create a more supportive environment and positive interactions.

One approach is to shift focus. Gently steering the conversation or activity toward a topic of interest to the individual can be highly effective. For example, asking questions like, "What's your favorite game?" or "Can you tell me about your favorite animal?" can help divert their attention away from stressors and engage them in a more enjoyable discussion.

Another technique involves engaging in calming activities. Introducing simple, soothing activities such as drawing, listening to music, or playing with a sensory toy can provide a distraction that helps to soothe their emotions. These activities can serve as a calming outlet, allowing individuals to focus on something enjoyable and less stressful.

In addition, using positive reinforcement is crucial. Acknowledging and praising their participation in the new focus encourages further engagement. For example, saying, "I love how you're drawing that! It looks great!" reinforces their involvement and helps them feel valued, which can promote a more positive experience.

Lastly, it's important to be patient. Allowing time for the individual to transition to the new focus is essential, as they may need a moment to shift their thoughts or feelings before fully engaging. Recognizing this need for time demonstrates respect for their process and a more understanding environment.

By employing gentle redirection, you can help individuals on the autism spectrum manage overwhelming emotions, creating a supportive atmosphere that encourages open communication. This technique not only develops a sense of safety but also enhances the overall interaction, making it more positive and effective.

Use Breaks

Suggest Pauses: Proposing breaks during high-emotion situations can be a valuable strategy for helping individuals on the autism spectrum regain composure. Effectively implementing this technique involves several key steps that can significantly improve interactions.

First, it's important to recognize signs of overwhelm. Pay attention to cues that indicate the individual may be feeling overwhelmed, such as fidgeting, frustration, or heightened anxiety. Identifying these signs early can help you intervene before emotions escalate further.

Once you've recognized the signs, you can offer a break. Calmly suggesting a short break can be beneficial. Phrases like, "How about we take a few minutes to breathe?" or "Let's step outside for a moment" can give the individual an opportunity to reset their emotions and regain their composure.

If possible, create a quiet space where they can relax without distractions. A calm environment can significantly aid in emotional regulation, allowing the individual to collect their thoughts and feelings in a safe setting.

During the break, you can encourage relaxation techniques. Suggesting simple calming methods, such as deep breathing or counting, can help the individual regain focus and calm. These techniques can provide them with effective tools to manage their emotions in the moment.

It is equally important to be patient and supportive. Let the individual know that it's okay to take a break and that you're there to support them. This reassurance can make a significant difference in how they perceive the situation, helping them feel more secure.

By incorporating breaks, you provide individuals with the time and space they need to process their emotions, which can lead to clearer thinking and a more constructive interaction moving forward.

These de-escalation techniques allow first responders, to cultivate a more supportive and understanding atmosphere when interacting with individuals on the spectrum. This thoughtful approach can lead to several positive outcomes:

First, it can enhance communication. By having a calm and respectful environment, officers improve clarity and understanding, making it easier for individuals to express themselves effectively.

Second, these techniques help reduce anxiety. Strategies such as validating feelings, offering choices, and suggesting breaks alleviates anxiety, allowing individuals to feel safer and more at ease.

A supportive approach can yield more effective outcomes. Not only does it improve the immediate interaction, but it also helps build trust and rapport, leading to better cooperation and understanding in future encounters.

Ultimately, these techniques empower officers to handle situations with empathy and sensitivity, ensuring that all individuals are treated with respect and dignity. This commitment can result in more positive experiences for individuals with autism and the community as a whole.

Chapter 5

Interactions During a Crisis/De-escalation

As first responders, we train and prepare for the worst, always hoping for the best. The nature of our work is that we often face high-stress, high-stakes situations, where every moment is critical. But what happens when the crisis we're responding to isn't violent or criminal in nature? What happens when the person we're trying to assist isn't in a place where they can hear us or respond to us the way we expect? When dealing with people in crisis, especially those on the autism spectrum, it's important to remember that things often go from bad to worse quickly, even when we are doing our best to stay calm and professional.

Autistic individuals, like many others, find comfort in routine and predictability. For them, routine is not just a preference, it's a necessity. When this routine is disrupted, it can send them into a state of heightened anxiety or stress. As first responders, we are often the ones who unintentionally disrupt that routine when we arrive on the scene. The very fact that we show up, lights flashing and sirens blaring, can be enough to cause a person on the autism spectrum to feel overwhelmed or even enter into a meltdown.

This is where our training in empathy, patience, and understanding comes into play. All we want as officers is to protect and serve the public, as we swore an oath to do. But doing this and remaining calm in the face of intense situations is not always easy. Sometimes, our own emotions are what need to be put in check first. This can be especially challenging when we are faced with behavior that we may not understand or that challenges our usual responses.

I can relate to this personally. I've faced many challenges with my daughter that have helped me gain a deeper understanding of how to approach situations with calmness and empathy. One experience that stands out to me occurred while my family was on a cruise ship. Traveling with an autistic child can be particularly difficult, as many environments and situations are simply not designed with their needs in mind. Thankfully, we were able to find a company called *Autism on the Seas*, which tailors cruise experiences for families like ours. However, not every moment on the trip was smooth, and one specific incident stands out as a reminder of how difficult these situations can be, and how important it is to stay composed.

During this particular episode, my daughter began having a meltdown. Something had triggered it, but in the moment, we weren't sure what. My instinct as a father was to try to help her calm down and regulate her emotions, but we were in a public area, and I needed to find a quiet space to help her manage the meltdown. As part of her self-regulation, my daughter often self-stimulates by biting herself. As much as I wanted to stop her, I knew that this was her way of coping, even though it was damaging. So, in an attempt to protect her from hurting herself, I instinctively placed my hand in front of her mouth, which she immediately latched on, biting me with great force. The pain from her bite was intense, and I could feel my emotions rise. At that moment, I wanted to react. My initial feeling was anger, frustration, and even a sense of helplessness. The pressure of her bite was so strong that it actually broke my finger.

But here's where the lesson came in: I knew that if I lashed out or reacted with anger, it would have only escalated the situation. If I had allowed my emotions to take control, I could have unintentionally caused harm, either physically or emotionally. Instead, I focused on maintaining control and keeping my voice steady. I worked to regulate my daughter as best as I could, remaining calm in the face of my own pain and frustration. It was a powerful reminder of how critical it is to manage our reactions in times of crisis.

Knowing my daughter never intended to harm me, I was still willing to place myself in that situation. As first responders we chose this profession, to place ourselves in situations that could potentially cause harm. Now, I'm not suggesting that officers should put themselves in harm's way or let themselves be hurt in order to de-escalate a situation. Our first and foremost goal is to go home to our own families. Instead what I am saying is that, in moments of crisis, especially with someone on the autism spectrum, understanding the person's behavior in the context of their struggle can help us respond more effectively. In this case, my daughter's behavior was not intentional; it was her way of trying to cope with a situation she couldn't control. And much like individuals on the autism spectrum, people in emotional or mental crisis often aren't acting out of malice, they're acting out of desperation, fear, confusion or extreme anxiety.

This is why, as first responders, it is crucial that we take a step back, assess the situation from a calm and clear perspective, and use our training to guide our response. Every situation is unique, but at its core, our job is to protect and serve with empathy. We need to remember that, often, the crisis isn't about the individual being "out of control"; it's about them being overwhelmed and unable to process what's happening. Our ability to communicate with them in a calm, non-threatening way can often be the difference between a situation escalating or being resolved peacefully.

As first responders, it's an inherent instinct for us, as well as for parents and human beings in general, to react immediately when we see someone engaging in behavior that we find undesirable by saying "no" or asking them to stop. This response comes naturally because we want to guide individuals towards acceptable behaviors and ensure their safety. However, in many cases involving children with autism, the behaviors may actually be attempts to seek attention. This means that our immediate reaction to intervene might inadvertently reinforce the behavior, especially if the child perceives the attention, whether positive or negative, as a reward.

Although it can be challenging, one of the most effective strategies in these situations is to ignore the unwanted behavior and instead redirect the child to a different, more appropriate activity. For example, consider a situation where a child with autism exhibits biting as an attention-seeking behavior. Directly responding to the biting by scolding or paying attention to it can unintentionally encourage the child to continue the behavior because they receive the interaction they were seeking.

The goal, therefore, becomes to gently guide the child towards an alternative activity that is not only engaging but also fulfills their need for interaction in a positive way. In the case of biting, this could involve offering a chewy toy that satisfies oral sensory needs or engaging them in a fun, interactive game that captures their interest. By shifting the focus from stopping the behavior to encouraging positive alternatives, we help the child learn more acceptable ways to gain attention and express themselves.

Crisis situations can be particularly challenging when interacting with individuals on the autism spectrum. Here are key strategies for handling these encounters.

Maintaining a calm composure during interactions is essential for creating a safer, more controlled environment. Here's how to keep a reassuring presence:

First, control your breathing by taking slow, deep breaths. This not only calms your own nerves but also helps you maintain composure, which helps reduce anxiety for both yourself and those around you.

Let your body language reflect calmness as well. Avoid tense postures, sudden movements, or expressions that might unintentionally escalate the situation. A relaxed stance communicates reassurance.

When speaking, use a soft, gentle tone. A calm voice can reduce the individual's anxiety, promoting a sense of safety and making it easier to connect without causing additional stress.

Manage your own emotional responses. If you start to feel overwhelmed, take a moment to pause and collect yourself before resuming the interaction. Staying aware of your own emotions allows you to respond thoughtfully rather than react impulsively.

Finally, keep your focus on de-escalation. Remember that your goal is to calm the situation, which will guide your actions and help you stay composed, even when challenges arise.

By following these steps, officers can help ease tension and create a supportive environment during their interactions.

Assessing the situation thoughtfully and thoroughly is essential in creating a safer environment and ensuring the well-being of everyone involved. Here's a comprehensive approach for quickly evaluating the scene and the overall situation.

Begin by surveying the scene for any immediate hazards. Scan the surroundings to identify potential risks, such as sharp objects, busy roads, bodies of water, fire, unstable structures, or uneven terrain. Spotting these dangers early allows you to take proactive steps to prevent harm and ensure safety. This quick assessment is especially critical in unpredictable or fast-paced situations, where sudden movements or a lack of awareness of certain dangers could increase the risk for the individual or bystanders. Environmental awareness is key to maintaining control and minimizing potential threats.

Next, monitor the individual's behavior closely. Look for signs that they may be experiencing distress or agitation. Changes in body language, unusual vocalizations, or repetitive movements might indicate they're feeling overwhelmed or struggling to cope with their surroundings. Some individuals may display behaviors that suggest self-harm or aggression toward others, which could escalate if not approached calmly.

Check for any immediate threats to safety, whether to the individual, nearby people, or yourself.

This includes being aware of behaviors that could lead to harm, such as attempts to flee into dangerous areas, physical aggression, or engaging with hazardous objects or substances. Recognizing these threats early helps you make informed decisions about whether immediate intervention is necessary.

Engage cautiously, approaching the individual calmly and observing their reaction to your presence. If you notice an increase in agitation, take a step back and reassess your approach to avoid coming across as a threat. A non-threatening demeanor can make a significant difference in calming the individual and creating an opportunity for connection.

Conducting this rapid, thoughtful evaluation allows officers to identify immediate safety concerns while minimizing the risk of escalation. This initial assessment provides a strong foundation for engaging in a way that is safe, empathetic, and effective.

Using simple, clear language when communicating can make a tremendous difference, especially in situations where confusion or misunderstanding could escalate stress. Here's a guide on how to communicate with clarity and purpose, ensuring instructions are easily understood.

Start by using direct and concise language. Keep sentences short and to the point to avoid overwhelming or confusing the individual. For instance, instead of saying, "I think it would be better if you sit down now," simply say, "Please sit down." Direct statements reduce ambiguity, making it easier for the person to understand your intentions and follow through with your instructions.

Avoid using jargon, technical terms, or any language that might be unfamiliar. Complex terms or professional language may be second nature to a responder but can be confusing or intimidating to someone in a stressful situation. Instead, use plain, everyday language. Clear, relatable words help convey your message in a way that feels approachable, increasing the likelihood that the individual can understand and respond appropriately.

Additionally, speak slowly and clearly. The natural response in high-stress situations is often to rush through communication, but doing so can make it harder for the individual to process what's being said. Take a calm, measured approach to speech, allowing for pauses when necessary, so the person has enough time to fully absorb each piece of information. Clear enunciation and a steady pace can make all the difference.

Sometimes, visual or physical cues can be invaluable. If the individual seems uncertain about verbal instructions, try pointing to an object or demonstrating the action you're requesting. For example, if asking someone to sit, gently gesturing toward a chair can reinforce your words and make your intention clearer. Visual cues are particularly helpful for individuals who struggle to process verbal information, providing an additional layer of clarity.

If the individual appears confused, calmly repeat key instructions using the same wording rather than rephrasing. Repetition, without changing the phrasing, can help reinforce understanding and avoid additional confusion that might arise from new or unfamiliar wording. Patience in repetition can be reassuring, showing the individual that they are being given time to comprehend without pressure.

By applying these communication strategies, first responders can create a calmer, more structured interaction. Simple, clear language reduces misunderstandings, helping the individual feel safer and more capable of following guidance, which ultimately contributes to a smoother and more positive outcome.

Prioritizing safety is a foundational step in managing challenging situations effectively, particularly when an individual may be in distress or overwhelmed. Ensuring that both the individual and everyone nearby are in a secure environment can help reduce risk, creating the foundation for a calmer more controlled interaction.

Once the area has been assessed, work to create a safe space. Clear the immediate surroundings of any objects or obstacles that might pose a danger or contribute to the individual's distress. Removing potential hazards, such as loose equipment, sharp tools, or unstable items, can help reduce the chances of accidental injury. A calm, uncluttered area allows the individual to feel more secure and reduces the likelihood of sudden movements or reactions that could escalate the situation.

If the individual is near a particular danger, such as a busy road, hazardous materials, or an overstimulating environment, guide them gently away from these risks. Approach slowly, using a calm tone, and encourage them to move to a quieter, safer location. Leading them to a less crowded area can help reduce their feelings of overwhelm caused by noise, movement, or other sensory input.

To further minimize overstimulation, turn off unnecessary sirens, flashing lights, or other intense stimuli if it's safe to do so. While these elements may be critical in emergencies, they can be highly distressing for individuals with sensory sensitivities, increasing anxiety and making communication more challenging. Loud noises, bright lights, and strong smells can contribute to further distress. By reducing sensory triggers and being mindful of the environment, you can create a calmer, more controlled atmosphere that fosters better communication and connection while respecting their needs.

Be mindful of your positioning, standing in a non-threatening posture and maintaining a safe distance. Avoid aggressive or defensive stances that could be interpreted as intimidating. Instead, adopt a relaxed posture that conveys approachability while keeping enough distance to ensure you're safe and prepared. Being alert to any sudden movements from the individual or bystanders enables you to respond swiftly if needed.

In the end, don't hesitate to engage with backup if the situation demands additional support. If handling the individual alone might be challenging, call for assistance from colleagues to help ensure everyone's safety. Having extra support can prevent potential escalation, but it's crucial to manage the presence of others carefully to avoid overwhelming or intimidating the individual.

By following these steps, first responders can help create a safer, more stable environment that reduces the potential for harm. Taking these careful, thoughtful actions prioritizes safety, providing a foundation for managing the situation calmly and effectively.

When managing difficult situations involving individuals who may be in distress, it is crucial to avoid forceful restraints whenever possible. Physical intervention should be a last resort, only used when absolutely necessary to ensure safety. Gentle guidance and a non-threatening approach can often be far more effective and help maintain a calm environment. Here's how to approach this in a respectful and safe manner.

First, assess the need for physical intervention carefully. Before considering any form of restraint, determine whether it is truly required to keep the individual safe. Whenever possible, try to de-escalate the situation verbally and use non-physical methods to guide the individual. Sometimes, a few calming words or simply allowing them a moment to regain composure can prevent the need for physical intervention entirely.

If gentle guidance becomes necessary, use a light, non-restrictive touch to direct the individual toward a safer area or away from potential hazards.

Rather than restraining, simply steer them with minimal contact, showing them where to move. A gentle touch can often convey reassurance and direction without creating additional stress. Remember that your goal is to guide, not to control, and that maintaining a calm, supportive presence is often the most effective approach.

During any physical intervention, communicate clearly and simply about what you're doing. Briefly explain your actions in plain language, such as, "I'm going to help you move over here." Using clear, straightforward terms helps the individual understand your intentions and feel more secure. This transparency can reduce confusion and make them feel more in control, especially if they are in a heightened state of anxiety or distress.

Throughout the interaction, maintain a non-threatening posture. Avoid standing too close or in a way that could be perceived as intimidating, such as looming over the individual. Instead, approach them at eye level if possible, and keep your body language open and relaxed. This approach helps reduce any potential fear or defensiveness, allowing them to respond more positively to your guidance.

If physical contact is unavoidable, use the absolute minimum force necessary to ensure everyone's safety. Avoid aggressive tactics or movements, and be prepared to release your hold as soon as it is safe to do so. Remember that any use of force can quickly increase the individual's stress or escalate the situation, so it is essential to be as gentle as possible and to reassess frequently.

Pay close attention to the individual's response to your intervention. Monitor their body language, vocalizations, and facial expressions to gauge their level of distress. If they appear to be more agitated, stop and consider adjusting your approach to one that better suits their comfort level. Sensitivity to their responses can help you adapt in real-time, providing reassurance and reducing the chance of escalation.

By following these guidelines, first responders can minimize the need for forceful restraints and manage situations effectively while respecting the individual's comfort and dignity. This approach not only leads to better outcomes but also a more positive experience for everyone involved, ultimately building trust and promoting safety.

Responding to Public Disturbances

When responding to disturbances involving individuals with autism, it is essential to take a more thoughtful and mindful approach. By prioritizing active listening, first responders can gain valuable insights into the situation before intervening, ensuring they address the individual's needs with sensitivity and understanding. Taking a moment to observe can reveal behaviors, expressions, and other cues that help to clarify what is occurring and why. This careful approach lays the groundwork for a more informed, compassionate response.

Begin by gathering as much information as possible. Before stepping in, observe the behaviors of both the individual and any others nearby. Notice who is present, what they're doing, and how they're interacting. Even small details can provide important context about the situation. Watching attentively can help you recognize patterns in the individual's behavior, especially if they're displaying signs of discomfort or distress. For example, an individual who is repeatedly covering their ears or avoiding eye contact may be overwhelmed by their surroundings. Taking the time to assess these subtleties allows you to make more informed decisions about how to proceed.

Non-verbal cues are often the most telling indicators of how an individual with autism is feeling. Body language, facial expressions, and even specific gestures can reveal their emotional state and comfort level. For instance, clenching fists or tensing up could indicate frustration, while rocking or repetitive movements may suggest self-soothing in response to sensory overload. By paying close attention to these signals, you can adapt your approach to help minimize stress and create a safer, more comfortable environment for everyone involved.

Active listening is crucial when interacting with the individual and anyone else present, such as family members, caregivers, or bystanders. Pay close attention to what is being said, including tone and pace, as these can provide valuable clues about the individual's emotional state and needs. Family members or caregivers may offer essential context, such as triggers for the disturbance or strategies that typically help calm the individual.

Engage respectfully with others by asking open-ended questions and acknowledging their perspectives. This can uncover critical insights about the individual's behavior and the events leading up to the situation. Listening attentively and including others in the process fosters empathy, builds rapport, and ensures a more effective and compassionate response.

As you observe and listen, try to identify any potential triggers. Triggers can range from environmental factors, such as loud noises, bright lights, or crowded spaces, to specific social interactions that might have caused distress. Recognizing these triggers can allow you to adjust your approach, for example, by moving the individual to a quieter area or reducing environmental stimulation. Taking the time to identify these factors shows the individual and those around them that their comfort and safety are your priorities.

By observing and listening carefully, first responders can gather the context they need to approach the situation with care and compassion. This informed perspective helps to de-escalate the disturbance, leading to a safer, more supportive environment for everyone involved.

Approaching with empathy is essential when interacting with individuals who may be overwhelmed or frightened. An empathetic approach allows first responders to communicate understanding and support, creating a foundation of trust and safety. By showing compassion and being attentive to the individual's emotional state, responders can help reduce stress and encourage cooperation in challenging situations.

Demonstrating understanding from the outset is a powerful way to build connection. Simple, empathetic statements like "I can see this is really upsetting for you" can validate the individual's emotions, showing that you're attuned to their experience. Acknowledging their feelings is not only supportive but also helps the individual feel seen and heard, which is crucial in moments of distress. This can be especially comforting for individuals who may feel isolated or misunderstood in their reactions to overwhelming stimuli or situations.

Maintaining a soft and reassuring tone can further reinforce feelings of safety. Speaking in a calm, gentle voice helps to soothe anxiety, signaling that you are there to help, not to harm. A loud or authoritative tone may increase stress, especially if the individual is already feeling vulnerable or overstimulated. By using a gentle approach, you convey patience and understanding, making it easier for the individual to respond positively.

Patience is key when offering empathy. Allow the individual ample time to process what's happening, and give them space to express themselves if they're able. Avoid interrupting or pressuring them to respond quickly, as processing emotions and information may take additional time. Being attentive and giving the individual room to communicate without interruption demonstrates respect for their experience and can reduce the intensity of the situation.

Non-threatening body language also plays an essential role in promoting a sense of security. Stand at a comfortable distance and maintain an open posture, such as keeping your hands visible and uncrossed. Avoid looming over the individual or standing too close, which may feel intimidating. Using a relaxed, open stance helps the individual feel safer and reduces the likelihood of further escalation, allowing for more constructive engagement.

Acknowledging that the individual may feel overwhelmed or fearful is another step in conveying empathy. Recognize the challenges they may be facing, whether it's sensory overload from a loud environment or anxiety from unfamiliar people or surroundings. By saying something like, "It's okay to feel scared," you validate their experience and help them understand that their feelings are normal, creating a comforting space for them to regain composure.

Offering support is crucial in an empathetic approach. A phrase like, "What can I do to help you right now?" invites collaboration and gives the individual a sense of control, which is often reassuring in stressful situations. This question shows that you're open to understanding their needs and willing to work with them toward a solution. Offering support in this way can also empower the individual to express their needs or desires, further helping to de-escalate tension.

Avoid jumping to conclusions or making assumptions about what the individual needs. Disturbances involving individuals with autism can arise from a variety of subtle or unseen factors. Instead of assuming, take the time to observe, ask questions, and listen carefully to their responses or the input of others. This patient and thoughtful approach allows you to interpret the situation accurately and respond with sensitivity. Misinterpreting their needs can increase frustration or fear, while actively seeking their perspective fosters respect, better communication, and more positive outcomes.

By approaching with empathy, first responders can show a sense of safety and calm. This empathetic connection can be transformative in de-escalating potentially volatile situations, creating a supportive environment where individuals feel secure, respected, and understood. The result is a more effective, compassionate response that improves outcomes for everyone involved.

Offering a safe space can be essential in de-escalating situations involving individuals who may feel overwhelmed or anxious.

The first step in helping someone regain control is to create a secure, quiet environment. Begin by identifying a nearby area that offers a break from the chaos, such as a side room, secluded hallway, or outdoor space with minimal noise and visual distractions. A calm setting provides a retreat from sensory triggers and allows the individual a momentary escape from the overwhelming intensity of the main environment.

Once a suitable location is found, gently guide the individual toward it using soft, non-threatening gestures and clear communication. Move slowly and avoid sudden actions that might startle or heighten their discomfort. Reassure them with calm, clear instructions about where you're going, fostering a sense of predictability and safety. Guiding someone to a peaceful space not only shows your commitment to their well-being but also helps prevent further escalation, allowing them to calm down and reestablish communication and trust.

As you lead them, using calming and encouraging language can reinforce a sense of security. Simple phrases like, "Let's go somewhere quieter where you can relax" or "You're safe with me; let's find a calm spot," can reassure them that the change is meant to help, not threaten. By framing the new environment as a place to feel safe, you increase the likelihood that they'll respond positively and view the relocation as a helpful measure rather than a forced move.

Allow the individual as much time as they need to settle into the space. Patience is critical, as they may need a few moments to adjust, take deep breaths, or just absorb the new surroundings. Avoid pushing for conversation or interaction right away; instead, give them the freedom to process the situation at their own pace. This breathing room often leads to a faster recovery, as they can self-regulate without feeling pressured to communicate immediately.

By offering a safe space in this way, first responders create an environment where individuals can feel more secure, significantly reducing the likelihood of escalation. This approach not only helps the individual regain their composure but also aids in trust and cooperation, contributing to a more effective and compassionate response.

Offer support if they indicate a need, but do so in a way that is calm and non-intrusive. Simple gestures, such as asking if they'd like a drink of water or offering them a seat, demonstrate care without overwhelming them. These thoughtful actions show your willingness to assist while respecting their personal space and avoiding added stress.

While giving them the space they need, remain close enough to offer reassurance and respond if they seek assistance. Let them know you're available to talk or help whenever they're ready. Your calm and patient presence signals respect for their needs while fostering a sense of trust and safety.

Engaging with patience

Patience is essential when engaging with individuals who may feel overwhelmed, anxious, or distressed. Allow them ample time to process the situation and gather their thoughts without rushing or pressuring them for quick answers, as this can increase their anxiety. Taking a calm, unhurried approach encourages respect and trust, helping them feel understood and more likely to express themselves clearly. This mindful engagement creates a pathway for meaningful dialogue and compassionate response.

Active listening is a cornerstone of patient engagement. When the individual begins to share their feelings or concerns, listen attentively. Simple, affirming gestures, such as nodding, maintaining eye contact, or using phrases like "I understand" or "Go on", demonstrate that you're genuinely engaged in what they're saying. These affirmations signal that their words are valued, encouraging them to open up further about their experiences.

Encouraging expression without forcing it is equally important. Open-ended questions like, "Can you tell me how you're feeling right now?" provide a gentle invitation for the individual to share their thoughts in their own words. This approach allows them to articulate their emotions at their own pace, fostering a sense of safety and comfort in the conversation.

Interrupting can disrupt this delicate process, so it's important to let the individual speak without interruption. By allowing them to express themselves fully, you communicate respect and give them the opportunity to share important insights. This uninterrupted space can be particularly beneficial for individuals who may struggle to articulate their feelings in high-stress situations, as it reassures them that they have your full attention.

As you listen, remain mindful of the individual's emotional state. Look for non-verbal cues; such as body language, facial expressions, or changes in tone, that may indicate their level of comfort or distress. Adjust your approach based on these cues to ensure you're meeting their needs effectively. If they appear increasingly anxious, consider adopting an even softer tone or giving them additional space to manage their emotions.

Maintaining a supportive and approachable presence is crucial during these interactions. Position yourself in a non-threatening manner, perhaps at eye level and at a respectful distance. This helps to convey a sense of safety and availability without making them feel crowded. The physical cues of support and approachability can be just as reassuring as verbal affirmations, providing a foundation for a trusting relationship.

Validating the individual's feelings can help normalize their emotions, making it easier for them to open up. Simple statements like, "It's okay to feel this way" or "I understand that this is difficult" acknowledge their experience and show empathy. When people feel that their feelings are understood and accepted, they are more likely to trust those around them, which can greatly improve the outcome of the interaction.

Offering reassurance is essential for easing the individual's anxiety. Remind them that they are safe and can take all the time they need to feel comfortable. Phrases like, "I'm here to help you; take as much time as you need," can be profoundly comforting, reinforcing that you are there to support them without pressure or urgency.

By engaging with patience and understanding, first responders can create an environment where individuals feel heard, respected, and valued. This approach not only reduces stress for everyone involved but also fosters effective, compassionate communication. Building a sense of safety and trust lays the foundation for more positive and constructive interactions, ensuring that the individual feels supported throughout the process.

Involving support personnel during interactions with individuals on the autism spectrum is crucial for ensuring effective communication and care. When trained professionals, such as mental health workers, social workers, or crisis intervention specialists, are available, they can play a vital role in managing the situation. These individuals bring specialized skills and knowledge that can help de-escalate potentially tense situations and provide tailored support. First responders should actively seek out these professionals when available to enhance the quality of their response.

It is essential to communicate clearly when introducing support personnel, outlining their roles and how they can assist. This transparency adopts a collaborative atmosphere and ensures that everyone involved is on the same page regarding the approach to the situation.

By working together, first responders, support personnel, and family members can develop a comprehensive plan tailored to the individual's needs. Open dialogue is key in finding the most effective strategies for support, as it allows everyone to contribute their perspectives. Respecting the individual's preferences regarding who they wish to involve in the situation is also crucial, as this can greatly affect their comfort level and overall response.

Facilitating communication between the individual and support personnel is another vital aspect of this approach. Support personnel may have already established a rapport with the individual, making it easier for them to express their thoughts and feelings. Sharing relevant background information about the individual's behavior or previous experiences can provide essential context that assists support personnel in understanding the current situation. First responders should monitor the interaction carefully, observing the individual's reactions to the involvement of support personnel and adjusting their approach as necessary to ensure comfort and safety.

By incorporating support personnel into their interventions, first responders can enhance the effectiveness of their responses and create a more supportive environment. This collaborative approach prioritizes understanding and care, ultimately leading to better outcomes for individuals on the autism spectrum and their families.

Enhancing Interactions with Individuals on the Autism Spectrum

By applying the outlined strategies, first responders and law enforcement officers can significantly improve their interactions with individuals on the autism spectrum. These approaches focus on understanding, compassion, and effective communication, which are essential in managing potentially challenging situations.

Promoting understanding is a cornerstone of these strategies. By recognizing the unique needs and behaviors of individuals with autism, first responders can approach each situation with empathy and respect. This understanding builds a supportive environment where individuals feel safe and heard.

Ensuring safety for all involved, including the individual with autism, their families, and responders themselves, is critical. Strategies such as assessing the situation, offering safe spaces, and involving support personnel contribute to minimizing risk and promoting de-escalation.

Building trust through engagement with families and caregivers of individuals with autism is essential for supporting positive relationships between the community and first responders. This proactive approach helps to alleviate fears and concerns that families may have regarding interactions with law enforcement. Regular outreach, community meetings, and informational sessions allow first responders to not only educate families about their roles and responsibilities but also to listen to the specific needs and challenges that families face. When families feel heard and understood, they are more likely to view law enforcement as allies rather than adversaries. This trust fosters an environment where individuals with autism can receive the support they need, ultimately leading to safer and more effective interactions during critical moments. Moreover, when families and caregivers see first responders actively working to understand and respect their experiences, it cultivates a sense of community and partnership that is essential for effective collaboration.

Chapter 6

Family Dynamics and Caregiver Support

Families and caregivers hold an indispensable place in the lives of autistic individuals, serving as their primary advocates, supporters, and sources of comfort. Their profound understanding and intimate knowledge of the unique needs, preferences, and challenges faced by those under their care make them vital participants in any interactions that involve first responders. This chapter explores the critical role that families and caregivers play and underscores the importance of collaboration between these key stakeholders and emergency responders.

The close relationships that caregivers have with autistic individuals equip them with insights that can immensely enhance the effectiveness of first responders during emergencies or routine interactions. From identifying triggers that might lead to anxiety or meltdowns, to suggesting communication techniques that work best with the individual, caregivers can provide guidance that ensures a more tailored and sensitive approach. By integrating caregivers into the response process, first responders not only gain valuable information but also promote an environment of trust and understanding.

Effective collaboration between first responders and caregivers requires intentional communication and mutual respect. Recognizing caregivers as partners rather than mere informants facilitates a cooperative dynamic that benefits all parties involved. This partnership can lead to the development of personalized strategies that consider the autistic person's unique profile, reducing the likelihood of distress and improving overall response outcomes.

The relationship between first responders and families should not end once an incident is resolved. Post-incident support and follow-up with caregivers are crucial to maintaining the trust and cooperation built during stressful events. Offering debriefing sessions, providing resources for ongoing care, and maintaining open lines of communication all contribute to a sustainable support network for families. Such continued collaboration ensures that caregivers feel empowered and supported, enhancing their ability to care for autistic individuals effectively while preparing them for any future interactions with emergency services.

Families and caregivers are not just peripheral to the lives of autistic individuals but are integral partners in ensuring their safety and well-being. By collaborating with family members, first responders can build a foundation for an inclusive approach that prioritizes the needs and voices of those who know autistic individuals best, thus creating a more compassionate and responsive community.

Understanding the Role of Families and Caregivers

Families and caregivers are fundamental in shaping the experiences and environment of autistic individuals. Their day-to-day involvement provides them with an intimate understanding of the unique needs, behaviors, and preferences of those in their care. This knowledge is invaluable, especially when it comes to guiding and improving interactions with first responders. By tapping into this resource, first responders can tailor their approaches to align with the specific sensitivities and communication needs of autistic individuals, ensuring that interactions are both respectful and effective.

In emergency situations or routine encounters, the input from families and caregivers can mean the difference between a challenging ordeal and a smoothly managed situation. For example, they might offer insights into specific triggers that could escalate stress, suggest comforting techniques that can help calm an individual, or provide effective methods of communication that the person responds well to. Scenarios where caregiver input has been leveraged often result in more positive outcomes, such as a reduced likelihood of distress and more efficient resolutions, highlighting the critical role that guardians play in these interactions.

Building collaborative partnerships with families is essential to maximizing the effectiveness of such engagements. Treating caretakers as partners rather than just informants establishes a dynamic of mutual respect and cooperation. This collaborative approach encourages the formulation of strategies that are informed by real-world experiences and the nuanced understanding that caregivers bring. Such partnerships not only enhance the immediate response to situations involving autistic individuals but also contribute to the development of protocols and strategies that are more likely to meet their needs in the long term.

The mutual benefits of engaging families and caregivers in this manner are profound. For caregivers, being actively involved and having their insights valued can lead to an increased sense of empowerment and assurance that their perspectives are respected in decision-making processes. For first responders, the collaboration results in access to a wealth of information that can refine their response strategies and improve outcomes. Ultimately, this partnership builds a strong foundation for trust and coordination, leading to a more supportive environment for autistic individuals, and lays the groundwork for ongoing cooperation that can adapt to new challenges and opportunities over time.

Overall, understanding and acknowledging the role of families and caregivers as active partners is crucial in advancing the effectiveness of interactions with autistic individuals. This collaborative spirit ensures that strategies are not only formed by professional training but are also enriched by experiences of those who know and support autistic individuals best, creating a more inclusive and adaptive approach to care and emergency response.

Effective Communication with Families

Effective communication with families and caregivers of autistic individuals is foundational to the success of any interaction involving first responders. It is essential to approach these interactions with a mindset that prioritizes respect and empowerment, recognizing the invaluable role that caregivers play in the lives of those they support. By ensuring that communication is both respectful and inclusive, first responders can build stronger, more trusting relationships with families, thereby enhancing outcomes during both routine and emergency situations.

To communicate effectively with caregivers, first responders should adopt practical strategies that respect their insights and expertise. This begins with recognizing caregtakers as partners and valuing their input as crucial to understanding the needs and behaviors of autistic individuals. Engaging advocates in a manner that is both respectful and empowering involves actively seeking their input and considering their perspectives in decision-making processes. This approach not only validates caregivers but also helps to alleviate their anxiety and stress, reinforcing their vital role in supporting the individual in question.

    Key communication techniques can significantly enhance the interaction between first responders and families. One such technique is active listening, where responders are fully present and attentive to the caregiver's words, minimizing interruptions and acknowledging their insights. This demonstrates genuine interest and concern, building rapport and trust. Additionally, using clear and straightforward language is crucial. Avoiding jargon and complex terminology ensures that caregivers can understand the information being shared, which is essential during potentially stressful situations where clarity is paramount.

Validation of caregiver concerns is another important aspect of effective communication. When caregivers express worries or fears, it is important for first responders to acknowledge these concerns and reassure the caregiver that their input is being considered seriously. This acknowledgement not only strengthens the trust between responders and families but also encourages an environment where caregivers feel comfortable sharing critical information that could aid in managing the situation effectively.

By implementing these communication strategies, first responders are better equipped to collaborate with families in a way that respects their role and contributions. This partnership is not merely transactional but rather a dynamic and ongoing relationship that brings better outcomes for autistic individuals and their communities. Overall, effective communication with families is about creating a supportive framework where caregivers feel heard, valued, and involved—ensuring that the needs of those they care for are comprehensively understood and met.

Engaging with Families and Caregivers

The effectiveness of law enforcement interactions can be significantly enhanced by actively involving families and caregivers. Encouraging family participation in discussions and decision-making processes allows responders to tap into the wealth of knowledge that families possess about their loved ones. As soon as it is appropriate, first responders should invite family members or caregivers to join the conversation, as their presence can often help de-escalate the situation and provide critical context.

Involving family members in decision-making empowers them. Asking questions like, "What do you think would be the best way to approach this?" encourages collaboration and ensures their perspective is considered. If multiple parties are involved, such as law enforcement and social services, clarifying each person's role helps the family know whom to communicate with and what to expect.

Provide Reassurance

Effective communication with families is critical during challenging situations. First responders should use straightforward and calm language to explain the circumstances and the actions being taken. It's vital to express intentions clearly, reassuring families that the primary goal is to support and protect their loved one. Simple statements like, "We are here to help" or "Your loved one's safety is our priority," can significantly alleviate anxiety and build trust.

Recognizing and validating the emotions that family members may experience, such as fear, worry, or frustration, is also essential. Phrases like, "I understand this is a stressful situation for you," can help families feel heard and respected. Maintaining transparency about the intervention process is equally important; being open about what to expect can further alleviate their concerns.

Encouraging families to ask questions develops a collaborative atmosphere and addresses any lingering doubts they may have. Regular updates on the situation and any changes are also beneficial, as they reassure families that responders are actively engaged in ensuring their loved one's safety.

Patience and compassion are necessary virtues when interacting with families during these times. First responders should be prepared to give families the time they need to process the situation and express their concerns. Following up after the incident can provide an opportunity for further support and reinforce the commitment to their loved one's well-being.

Share Information

When appropriate, first responders should share information about available resources or services for individuals with autism and their families. Before doing so, assessing the relevance of these resources to the current situation is critical to ensure they meet the individual's needs. Compiling a list of local resources, such as support groups, counseling services, and crisis intervention programs, specifically designed for individuals with autism, can be incredibly beneficial.

Providing contact information, including phone numbers, websites, and addresses for these organizations, allows families to reach out for assistance immediately if needed. Highlighting specific services, such as local crisis intervention teams or therapeutic services, can provide families with a clearer understanding of what resources are available to them.

Encouraging families to utilize these resources emphasizes that support is available to help them navigate the challenges they may face.

It's essential to be sensitive to the timing of when this information is shared. Families may feel overwhelmed during a crisis, so offering resources after the immediate situation has been addressed can be more effective. Following up later to see if the family utilized any of the provided resources can demonstrate ongoing support and care.

First responders should always remain available for any questions or further assistance regarding these resources, ensuring that families feel empowered and informed.

Respecting family dynamics is paramount in creating a supportive environment for individuals on the autism spectrum. Each family has unique dynamics, beliefs, and communication styles. First responders should approach each family as an individual unit, avoiding general assumptions. Practicing cultural sensitivity and being aware of the family's cultural background can also inform the support provided, allowing for a more tailored approach.

Adapting communication styles based on the family's preferences is crucial. Some families may prefer direct communication, while others may benefit from a gentler or more indirect approach. Understanding the power dynamics within a family is also vital; certain members may have more influence in decision-making, and recognizing this can help guide interactions more effectively.

Encouraging family members to share their perspectives fosters an inclusive atmosphere where everyone feels valued. Phrasing questions like, "How would you like us to approach this?" demonstrates respect for their insights. It's essential to avoid stereotyping and discrimination. Treat each family uniquely to build trust and rapport.

By maintaining a neutral and non-judgmental stance, first responders can create an environment of trust. This approach encourages collaboration and enhances the effectiveness of the response.

Following up with families or caregivers after a situation has been resolved demonstrates genuine care and commitment to their well-being. Initiating contact with a simple phone call, email, or visit can show that the responder is invested in the family's post-incident experience. Expressing concern for both the individual and the family's overall well-being helps solidify this bond.

Asking about their needs after the incident reinforces a commitment to support. This inquiry can lead to additional resources or assistance, ensuring the family feels heard and cared for. If further resources were not shared during the initial interaction, following up provides an excellent opportunity to do so.

Encouraging open communication is essential for maintaining trust. Families should feel comfortable reaching out with any questions or concerns in the future. Gathering feedback from families on their experiences can provide valuable insights for improving future interactions.

Documenting follow-up interactions, including feedback received, can guide future practices and enhance overall effectiveness. Expressing gratitude to families for their cooperation during the situation strengthens relationships and fosters goodwill.

Following up after an incident not only demonstrates ongoing support but also enhances trust between first responders and families. This proactive approach can lead to better outcomes for individuals with autism and their loved ones, advocating a collaborative relationship that benefits everyone involved.

Supporting Caregivers Post-Incident

Supporting caregivers following an incident involving autistic individuals is a crucial aspect of ensuring effective collaboration and long-term trust between families and first responders. The aftermath of any incident can be a period of heightened stress and uncertainty for caregivers, who often must process emotional and logistical challenges. Providing continued support post-incident not only affirms the commitment of responders to the well-being of the families involved but also strengthens the foundation for future collaboration. This ongoing support is essential in maintaining the trust that is built during the initial response and reassures caregivers that they are not alone in managing the complexities they face.

Follow-up support can be implemented through a variety of strategies, starting with debriefing sessions that involve caregivers in discussions about the incident. These sessions provide an opportunity to openly share experiences, discuss what transpired, and address any lingering concerns or questions. Such interactions allow caregivers to offer feedback, which can be invaluable for responders seeking to improve their practices. Importantly, more these discussions help caregivers feel that their voices are heard and that they are valued partners in the management and resolution of incidents.

Beyond immediate debriefing, the provision of resources and referrals to support networks or services is another critical strategy for post-incident support. Referring caregivers to relevant support groups or service providers can help them receive the emotional and logistical assistance they need during the aftermath of an incident. Access to specialized counseling, autism advocacy organizations, or family support services can ease the burden on caregivers, offering them guidance and a sense of community as they navigate these challenges. By facilitating access to these resources, first responders demonstrate their commitment to holistic support that goes beyond the immediate incident.

Building long-term relationships with caregivers is perhaps the most enduring form of support that can be offered. When they know that there is a reliable network of support they can turn to during stressful times, it cultivates an ongoing relationship rather than a purely transactional one. This can be achieved by maintaining regular communication with families, checking in on their well-being, and inviting them to participate in community events or training sessions. Long-lasting partnerships are built on trust, understanding, and mutual respect, and they ultimately contribute to creating a supportive environment where autistic individuals and their families feel safe and valued.

Overall, supporting advocates post-incident involves a comprehensive approach that addresses their immediate concerns and lays the groundwork for continued collaboration. By prioritizing follow-up support, strategies for feedback and resource provision, and the development of long-term relationships, first responders can enhance the effectiveness of their interventions and contribute positively to the communities they serve.

The Unseen Struggles: Parenting on the Spectrum

When it comes to autism, there are many struggles that go unnoticed behind the scenes, struggles that even first responders will never witness or fully understand. This hidden reality becomes even more apparent when considering a recent study that found nearly 1 in every 5 parents of a child on the autism spectrum has Post-Traumatic Stress Disorder (PTSD). To put this into perspective, the prevalence of PTSD among combat veterans is 1 in every 14. This stark comparison highlights the immense and often unacknowledged stresses and concerns faced by parents of autistic children and the parallels in the high-stress environments shared with first responders.

The ongoing fears are relentless. Parents constantly worry about scenarios such as, "What if my child runs into traffic? What if they wander outside and never return? What traumas might they have endured that they cannot express to me?" These are not just fleeting thoughts, but persistent fears rooted in the realities of raising a child on the spectrum. My own daughter has runaway from me into traffic, just after walking out of a grocery store, all while laughing her heart out.

I remember one particularly harrowing experience during a cruise with *Autism on the Seas*. While disembarking at one of the ports, our daughter suddenly decided she wanted to go swimming and darted towards the edge of the pier, ready to jump into the ocean. Thankfully, I had a leash attached to both her wrist and mine and was able to pull her back just in time, preventing a potential tragedy. Moments like this underscore the constant vigilance required of parents like me and my wife.

To put this in perspective, as first responders, we are trained to play the "what if" game. We anticipate and prepare for potential outcomes, but for many of us, that game ends when we go home. For parents of autistic children, however, this game is never-ending. It's a constant mental exercise, a loop that plays out every moment of every day. And if you think it might pause at night, think again.

One time, while camping in Yellowstone National Park, my daughter woke up at 2 a.m. and attempted to run outside the trailer. Thankfully, I had taken extra precautions to secure the door and heard her trying to open it, which woke me up. That night, I stayed awake with her, sitting in front of the door while she paced back and forth inside the trailer stimming and watching *My Little Pony*, as I sat there in the darkness, haunted by thoughts of what might have happened if she had managed to get out. Would she have been attacked by a bear, a wolf, or a bison? Would she have wandered into the woods, becoming lost and unable to navigate her way back or communicate with anyone who tried to help? What if she went down to the river, fell in and drowned? The possibilities were endless, and each was terrifying.

These incidents shape the fears that parents carry every single day. They are why so many parents take what may seem like extreme precautions, not to be overbearing or "helicopter parents," but to protect their children from harm. For parents of children on the autism spectrum, the stakes are high, and the margin for error is non-existent. This reality shapes our lives, our routines, and our interactions with the world around us. The world can be a challenging place to navigate on its own. Add autism into the mix, along with people who choose not to understand, and it becomes even more difficult.

Understanding this allows first responders to bridge a gap to create empathy. Recognizing the immense pressures and fears that parents endure can help foster a deeper connection and more effective support for families navigating the challenges of autism. After all, the unseen battles they face are just as significant as the ones we encounter on the job.

Conclusion

It's crucial for first responders to reflect on the things discussed in this chapter, improving interactions with autistic individuals and their caregivers. The involvement of families and caregivers stands as a cornerstone to successful interventions. Their unique insights and understanding of the autistic individual's behaviors and needs are invaluable resources that can significantly enhance the effectiveness of first responder actions. Through effective communication strategies, where active listening, clarity, and validation are prioritized, a foundation of trust and respect is built. These strategies not only improve the immediate outcomes during interactions, but also contribute to a long-term positive relationship between first responders and families.

In addition, the importance of ongoing support systems cannot be overstated. By implementing robust follow-up procedures and providing access to resources and community support networks, first responders can ensure that caregivers feel supported even after the initial incident has been resolved. This holistic approach not only addresses immediate needs but also empowers caregivers, providing them with tools and systems that help them better manage future challenges and reduce anxiety associated with crisis situations.

Moving forward, it is essential to translate these insights into actionable steps. This chapter calls upon first responders and community stakeholders to adopt and prioritize these practices as standard protocol. Establishing comprehensive training and education programs can equip first responders with the skills necessary to engage effectively and empathetically with autistic individuals and their families. Institutions should also invest in developing partnerships with autism organizations, which can offer invaluable resources and insights into best practices.

By making these strategies a standard part of first responder training and community engagement efforts, we not only enhance the safety and well-being of autistic individuals but also reinforce the support structure for their families and caregivers. As stakeholders in the communities they serve, first responders have the power to effect meaningful change and set an example for other sectors to follow. Let this be a call to action for building a more inclusive, understanding, and supportive environment where every individual is treated with dignity and respect, and where caregivers feel valued and supported in their crucial roles.

Chapter 7

Collaboration with Autism Organizations

In the previous chapter, I touched briefly on the significant impact that specialized services like *Autism on the Seas* (AOTS) can have for families like ours, who are navigating the unique challenges of traveling with a child on the autism spectrum. The personalized care and understanding provided by AOTS were truly transformative for our family, but there is one particular moment from our trip that has stayed with me, one that changed the way I view the world and our journey as a family.

When we first decided to travel with *Autism on the Seas*, we were filled with uncertainty. My daughter, who has been nonverbal for most of her life, faces daily struggles with communication and sensory overload. As a father, I've often found myself wishing I could do more to help her feel understood, to offer her a sense of relief and peace in a world that can sometimes be overwhelming. So, when we embarked on that cruise, I wasn't sure what to expect, but what I received was nothing short of a life-changing experience.

From the moment we boarded, we were greeted with warmth and kindness. The priority boarding was a relief, helping to reduce the stress of crowded areas and long waits. But it wasn't just the logistical ease of the trip that made it special, it was the genuine care and support from the staff. The volunteers who work with *Autism on the Seas* aren't just there to assist; they're there to truly connect. They took the time to learn about our family's unique needs, showing empathy and understanding that went far beyond what we could have hoped for. It felt like they were part of our journey, not just a service we were paying for.

But the most profound moment of all came toward the end of the trip, when my daughter, who had never spoken these words to me before, turned to me and said, "Thank you, Dad." Those words, simple, yet profound, were a gift I'll treasure forever. To hear her express gratitude in her own way, after a vacation that allowed her to feel seen, heard, and cared for in a way that was tailored to her needs, was an emotional breakthrough. In that moment, I understood the power of these experiences, and how much they can change not only the lives of those directly affected but the entire family dynamic.

The vacation wasn't just about getting away from everyday life; it was about creating a space where my daughter could thrive in ways she hadn't before. The one-on-one support allowed me to step back for a moment, to experience the joy of watching her enjoy herself without the usual stresses that come with traveling. It wasn't just about the excursions or the vacation itself; it was about the emotional growth we all experienced, as a family, in a place where we felt fully supported and accepted.

That "thank you, Dad" will be something I carry with me every single day. It was a reminder that moments of joy and connection, however small, are life-changing for us as parents. *Autism on the Seas* gave us not just a vacation but the chance to create new memories, to deepen our bond, and to experience something as a family that many people take for granted, the ability to simply enjoy each other's company in an environment that feels safe and inclusive.

Now, when I think back to that trip, I realize just how deeply it impacted our lives. It wasn't just a break from routine, it was a transformative experience that allowed us to grow, to laugh, and to understand each other better. And most importantly, it gave my daughter the opportunity to express herself in a way she hadn't before, showing me how powerful a thoughtful, supportive environment can be in helping someone reach new heights of communication and connection.

Every day, I cherish those words my daughter spoke to me, because they represent a moment of pure connection, one that I'll never forget. For that, I am forever grateful to *Autism on the Seas*, who helped make this unforgettable experience possible for our family.

But the impact of this journey extends far beyond just our own family. Since that trip, I've had the privilege of working with other families, many of whom are struggling with the same challenges we face. I've been out in the field, listening to parents vent their frustrations about feeling stuck, overwhelmed, and unsure of where to turn for support. As someone who has been in the trenches and understands those feelings, I've made it a point to share our experience with *Autism on the Seas*, and the difference it has made in our lives. To my surprise, many of these families had never heard of such specialized services, and after learning about it, it completely changed their perspective on what was possible for their own vacations.

There are so many incredible community organizations throughout the nation, and within our own local communities, that offer support to families with autistic individuals. Sometimes, all it takes is a little guidance to help families find the right resources that can truly make a difference. It's easy to feel like you're navigating the world alone, but the truth is, there are so many avenues of help and support out there. It's about knowing where to look, and sometimes, just being able to point someone in the right direction can change their lives.

I've seen firsthand how something as simple as learning about *Autism on the Seas* can open up a world of possibilities for families who feel trapped or isolated in their struggles. And that's just one example of the many resources available to us. The journey isn't always easy, but it's reassuring to know that help is out there, often closer than we realize. If we can shine a light on these resources, we can help create opportunities for families to not only survive but thrive. That's something we should all strive for.

Building Partnerships with Local Advocacy Groups

Establishing relationships with local autism advocacy groups can significantly enhance law enforcement's understanding and effectiveness in engaging with individuals on the autism spectrum. By fostering these connections, first responders can develop crucial insights that improve their interactions and responses to the unique needs of this community. Below are several steps to effectively research and establish connections with local autism organizations, ensuring that first responders are well-equipped to serve and support individuals with autism.

Identify Local Organizations

For first responders, identifying and connecting with local autism advocacy groups and related organizations is critical for enhancing response capabilities and community relations. To begin, thorough research is essential. First, use online resources such as directories, social media platforms, and websites dedicated to autism support to find local organizations like the Autism Society or other regional chapters of national groups. Additionally, checking community listings can yield valuable information; local community boards, libraries, and social service agencies often maintain directories of nonprofits and advocacy groups focused on autism.

Another key avenue is to engage with local health and education systems. By contacting schools and educational institutions, first responders can tap into the networks of special education departments that frequently collaborate with advocacy organizations for resources and training. Furthermore, healthcare providers, including hospitals and mental health professionals, can offer insights into local autism resources and support networks, facilitating a comprehensive understanding of the community's needs.

Attend Local Events and Meetings

Attending local events and meetings organized by autism advocacy groups is a proactive approach to building partnerships. First responders should participate in community events such as workshops, support groups, and awareness days. This not only establishes networking opportunities but also demonstrates a commitment to community engagement. Joining local task forces or committees focused on disability services can also be beneficial, as it keeps first responders informed and connected with the evolving landscape of autism support in their area.

Networking with other first responders can further enhance these efforts. By sharing resources and contacts, paramedics, firefighters, and police officers can collaborate to strengthen their collective understanding of local autism organizations. Creating a coalition of first responders dedicated to researching and engaging with autism advocacy groups allows for a unified approach in serving the community effectively.

Establish Communication Channels

Once local organizations are identified, establishing communication channels is the next critical step. Initiating contact through email, phone calls, or in-person meetings allows first responders to introduce themselves and express interest in collaboration. Requesting meetings with the leadership of these organizations can lead to fruitful discussions regarding potential partnerships, training opportunities, and how law enforcement can actively support their mission.

Staying informed and updated is equally important. Subscribing to newsletters offered by advocacy groups ensures that first responders remain aware of community needs and upcoming events. Engaging with these organizations on social media can further enhance connections and maintain awareness of their activities, building a sense of community involvement.

Promote Collaborative Efforts

Building collaborative efforts with local autism organizations is essential for establishing effective partnerships. Developing formal partnerships allows for resource sharing, joint training initiatives, and improved service delivery. Offering to co-host training sessions or workshops is a valuable strategy to educate first responders on autism awareness, communication strategies, and effective intervention techniques. These collaborative efforts can lead to more informed and compassionate responses when interacting with individuals on the autism spectrum.

Participate in Community Events

Participating in community events organized by autism advocacy groups is a significant opportunity for first responders. These events serve as platforms to enhance understanding, build relationships, and demonstrate commitment to supporting the community. Strategies for effective participation include identifying relevant events by monitoring local calendars, community bulletin boards, and social media for upcoming autism awareness days, workshops, seminars, and training sessions. Connecting with autism organizations to learn about their event schedules can also facilitate meaningful participation.

Planning ahead is crucial to ensure adequate personnel can attend events without compromising emergency response capabilities. Preparing materials, such as informational brochures about autism and first responder services, can enhance community outreach. Engaging actively in the event activities, including workshops and training sessions, not only provides valuable learning opportunities but also shows community members that first responders are genuinely invested in understanding autism.

Collaborate and Document Participation

Collaborating with autism organizations can further strengthen relationships. Co-hosting events or inviting experts to speak at workshops can enrich the experience for both first responders and community members. Documenting participation through photos and stories shared on social media or internal newsletters can highlight the department's commitment to community engagement and promote goodwill. Gathering feedback from participants after events can also provide insights into their perspectives, helping to shape future initiatives.

By actively researching and connecting with local autism advocacy groups, first responders can gain invaluable resources, enhance their skills, and develop stronger relationships with the autism community. These efforts ultimately lead to more effective and compassionate responses to individuals on the autism spectrum, ensuring that law enforcement serves as a supportive ally in the community.

Benefits of Participation

Participation in community events organized by autism advocacy groups offers numerous benefits to first responders, significantly enhancing their ability to serve and support individuals on the autism spectrum. One of the most important advantages is the opportunity to build community trust. By attending these events, first responders demonstrate their commitment to understanding and supporting individuals with autism and their families. This dedication not only helps to establish a positive relationship but also encourages open dialogue within the community. When individuals feel comfortable communicating with first responders, it becomes easier for them to reach out during times of need, ultimately leading to more effective interactions.

Furthermore, participation enhances knowledge and skills among first responders. Engaging directly with individuals with autism and their families provides valuable insights into their unique challenges and needs. This firsthand learning experience can lead to improved awareness and a greater understanding of autism. Additionally, workshops and training sessions offered at these events can equip first responders with best practices for communicating and interacting with individuals on the spectrum. As they gain this knowledge, they become better prepared to respond compassionately and effectively in various situations.

Strengthening community relations is another critical benefit of participation in autism events. By promoting inclusivity, first responders help foster a sense of belonging for individuals with autism and their families. Their presence at these events signals that the community values and supports its diverse members. Additionally, engaging with autism organizations and community members facilitates networking opportunities that can lead to collaborative efforts benefiting both the first responders and the autism community. Such partnerships can improve service delivery and create a more supportive environment for everyone involved.

Moreover, participation encourages continuous improvement within law enforcement practices. Insights gained from community events can inform policies and practices, ensuring they are more effective and compassionate toward individuals with autism. This engagement furthers a culture of lifelong learning, where first responders are motivated to continue their education and adapt their approaches to better serve individuals on the autism spectrum. By embracing these opportunities for growth, law enforcement can contribute positively to the overall welfare of the community.

Engaging in Dialogue

Open communication between first responders and autism advocacy groups is essential for understanding the challenges individuals with autism face. Regular meetings with advocacy groups provide a platform to discuss critical issues, such as effective communication strategies and the unique needs of the autism community. Involving diverse stakeholders, including families, experts, and individuals with autism, enriches the conversation and helps law enforcement gain a broader perspective.

Creating a safe space for dialogue, practicing active listening, and discussing specific challenges and success stories amplifies trust and collaboration. Developing action plans together ensures that discussions lead to actionable strategies, and setting measurable goals helps track progress. Encouraging community feedback through surveys or forums enhances law enforcement practices and ensures that multiple perspectives are considered.

Benefits of Engaging in Dialogue

Engaging in dialogue offers numerous benefits, including a deeper understanding of autism, which improves law enforcement interactions with individuals on the spectrum. This increased awareness increases empathy, reduces misunderstandings, and promotes effective communication. Building trust within the community also encourages cooperation, making individuals and families more likely to seek help from law enforcement.

Dialogue also enhances service delivery by tailoring responses to meet the specific needs of individuals with autism, reducing the potential for escalation in tense situations. Collaborative efforts with autism advocacy groups can lead to joint training and outreach initiatives, strengthening community support and fostering a more inclusive environment for everyone involved.

Collaborative Training: Enhancing Understanding of Autism for First Responders

Collaborative training between first responders and autism advocacy organizations is key to improving understanding and communication when interacting with individuals on the spectrum. These sessions equip law enforcement with essential tools for effective engagement, tailored to the unique needs of the autism community. Training should be informed by assessments of specific skill gaps, with input from advocacy groups to ensure relevance. Customized programs, using various methods like workshops, role-playing, and case studies, enhance learning and accommodate different learning styles.

Involving autism experts, including educators and families, enriches the training by providing real-world insights and perspectives. Practical exercises such as scenario simulations and sensory overload drills help officers gain hands-on experience in controlled environments. Continuous improvement is achieved by regularly gathering feedback from participants to assess effectiveness and adapt content accordingly. Ongoing training makes for a proactive approach to autism awareness, keeping law enforcement informed on best practices.

The benefits of collaborative training are numerous. It increases understanding of autism's communication styles, sensory sensitivities, and behavioral challenges, promoting empathy and effective de-escalation strategies. Officers gain confidence through hands-on experience, improving their ability to handle high-stress situations. This approach strengthens community trust by showing law enforcement's commitment to inclusivity, while also establishing stronger community relations through collaborative efforts with advocacy groups.

Resources for Training and Support

Investing in specialized training programs is vital for law enforcement to improve interactions with individuals on the autism spectrum. Training should be tailored to specific needs identified through surveys and consultations with autism advocacy organizations. The curriculum should focus on key areas such as communication techniques, sensory sensitivities, and de-escalation strategies, using a combination of interactive workshops, role-playing, and online resources for flexible learning.

Incorporating feedback after each session ensures continuous improvement, while peer learning encourages knowledge sharing. Online platforms such as Autism Speaks and the International Association of Chiefs of Police offer valuable resources like webinars, courses, and case study discussions to support ongoing education. Regularly engaging with these resources helps officers stay informed and enhances their ability to respond appropriately.

By investing in comprehensive training programs and online resources, law enforcement can improve their effectiveness in dealing with individuals with autism, creating trust and a safer, more inclusive environment for all.

Implementing Simulation Exercises and Engaging Support Networks for First Responders

Simulation exercises are an essential tool for preparing first responders to interact with individuals on the autism spectrum. These hands-on, scenario-based training sessions provide a controlled environment where officers can practice key skills such as communication and recognizing sensory sensitivities. By collaborating with autism experts and advocacy organizations, realistic scenarios can be created, reflecting common situations like welfare checks, traffic stops, or behavioral crises. These simulations allow officers to refine their responses and build confidence.

Training materials should include detailed scenarios with role-playing guidelines, along with props or technology to enhance realism. First responders can then engage in simulations with trained actors or volunteers portraying individuals with autism. Facilitators guide the exercises and conduct debriefing sessions afterward to discuss feedback and improve future training. This feedback loop helps refine scenarios and ensures the training remains relevant and effective. Regular simulation sessions reinforce skills, while peer learning promotes knowledge sharing among officers.

Additionally, connecting first responders with support networks like local autism organizations and national groups such as Autism Speaks can further enhance their understanding and skills. Law enforcement agencies can establish partnerships with these organizations, offering opportunities for officers to attend workshops and network events. Encouraging officers to participate in support group meetings and mentorship programs strengthens relationships and broadens their knowledge.

Engaging with online platforms like social media groups, webinars, and discussion forums provides ongoing learning and up-to-date strategies. Collecting feedback from support networks enables agencies to adapt training programs, improving first responders communication, empathy, and overall interactions with individuals on the autism spectrum. By integrating simulation exercises and insights from these networks, agencies foster a more informed, compassionate response, ultimately enhancing community relations and the effectiveness of their teams.

Sensory bags for First Responders

As first responders, a powerful way to support the autistic community is by equipping patrol vehicles, fire rigs, and ambulances with sensory bags. These bags, designed to provide comfort and reassurance, can be invaluable during emergencies. Having a sensory bag readily available ensures that you can offer immediate aid tailored to the unique needs of an autistic individual, potentially preventing sensory overload or a meltdown during highly stressful situations.

Consider this example: if I were involved in a vehicle accident and rendered unconscious or even fatally injured, my daughter might survive but face significant challenges. She could be hiding injuries due to her high pain tolerance or struggling with the overwhelming stimuli around her. A sensory bag provided to her in that moment might not solve every problem, but it could make a critical difference by offering tools to manage her sensory needs and feel a sense of control amidst the chaos.

By incorporating sensory bags into standard emergency equipment, first responders can extend their ability to care for vulnerable individuals in distress.

Suggested Items for a Sensory Bag

To create a sensory bag that meets diverse needs, consider including:

Noise-Canceling Headphones or Earplugs: Helps reduce overwhelming sounds like sirens or crowds.

Fidget Toys: Stress balls, spinners, or squishy toys to provide a calming outlet for nervous energy.

Weighted Lap Pad or Blanket: Offers a sense of security through deep pressure stimulation.

Sunglasses or Tinted Glasses: Reduces sensitivity to bright lights.

Chewable Jewelry or Chewy Tubes: Provides a safe outlet for oral sensory needs.

Comfort Items: Small plush toys or soft fabrics that feel soothing to the touch.

Visual Aids: Laminated emotion cards or a simple picture board for nonverbal communication.

Snacks and Water: Non-perishable, sensory-friendly snacks like crackers or applesauce pouches.

Calming Smells: Lavender or chamomile sachets (ensure the scent is mild and not overpowering).

Small Flashlight with Filters: Allows control over light brightness and color, reducing harsh lighting.

Bubble Timer or Liquid Motion Toy: Provides a visually calming distraction.

Hand Sanitizer or Wipes: For hygiene needs, as cleanliness can be comforting for some.

Blank Notebook and Crayons: Encourages expression through drawing or writing.

By adopting sensory bags as part of your standard protocol, you can demonstrate empathy, understanding, and a proactive approach to assisting the autistic community during emergencies.

Benefits of Hosting Community Forums

Hosting community forums is a key strategy for building trust between law enforcement and the communities they serve, particularly in understanding autism spectrum disorder (ASD) and the challenges faced by individuals with autism. These forums encourage transparency, accountability, and open dialogue, promoting empathy and collaboration. By allowing community members to share their experiences and advocate for their needs, forums help foster a more cohesive, informed, and supportive community for individuals with autism and their families.

Creating Effective Feedback Mechanisms

Implementing feedback mechanisms is crucial for law enforcement to gather insights from families of individuals with autism, helping to improve practices and interactions. These mechanisms can include surveys, online feedback forms, and mobile apps, making it easier for community members to share their experiences. Hosting focus groups specifically for families offers a deeper understanding, while anonymous reporting options encourage honest feedback without fear of repercussions. Engaging community advocates and partnering with autism organizations further promotes participation. Additionally, a follow-up system to acknowledge and act on feedback demonstrates responsiveness, contributing to continuous improvement in law enforcement practices.

Collaborating on Autism Awareness Events

Partnering with autism organizations to create awareness events promotes understanding and acceptance. A successful events starts by identifying shared goals, focusing on the specific challenges individuals with autism face during law enforcement interactions. Collaborating on these objectives ensures the events is targeted and effective in addressing key issues.

Creating educational content is essential for autism awareness events. By developing materials that explain autism and incorporating personal stories, the message becomes more humanized, allowing the community to connect with the experiences of individuals on the spectrum. Platforms like social media and community events are crucial for engaging the public and fostering meaningful dialogue. These events can include a variety of activities such as golf tournaments, car shows, sensory events, and motorcycle rides, all providing opportunities to raise awareness in unique and engaging ways.

Joint training programs are also a key component, equipping law enforcement with the skills needed to communicate effectively with individuals on the spectrum. Involving community stakeholders, such as local leaders and various groups, broadens the events' reach and promotes inclusivity, helping to create a more understanding environment for individuals with autism.

Measuring the impact of these initiatives is vital for ongoing improvement. Gathering feedback and assessing the effectiveness of each event helps refine future efforts. Promoting ongoing awareness through updated materials and showcasing successes ensures that these initiatives remain impactful, continually educating and engaging the community in a long-term commitment to support individuals on the spectrum.

By prioritizing these initiatives, law enforcement can enhance their understanding of autism, improve interactions, and foster a culture of inclusivity within the community.

Benefits of Collaborating on Awareness Events

Collaborating on awareness events is an effective strategy for law enforcement agencies to enhance community understanding and acceptance of individuals with autism. Such events not only educate the public about autism and its associated challenges but also promote stronger relationships between law enforcement and the autism community. This partnership builds trust and cooperation, ultimately leading to improved interactions during encounters with law enforcement.

Increased understanding is one of the primary benefits of awareness events. By educating the community about autism, these initiatives create an understanding of empathy and compassion, allowing residents to better understand the unique challenges faced by individuals on the spectrum and their families. Law enforcement personnel also benefit from enhanced preparedness through targeted training sessions included in these events. Officers gain the necessary skills and knowledge to effectively interact with individuals with autism, resulting in more positive outcomes during encounters.

Engaging the community in awareness efforts empowers individuals and families affected by autism, encouraging them to advocate for their needs and promote acceptance. By working together, first responders can significantly improve community interactions with individuals on the autism spectrum.

This proactive approach constructs a culture of inclusivity and support within the community.

Building Trust Through Success Stories and Collaboration

Highlighting positive interactions between law enforcement and individuals with autism is a powerful way to build community trust and encourage cooperation. Success stories inspire others and educate the public on law enforcement's dedication to understanding autism. Law enforcement agencies can gather these stories through officer, family, and autism organization submissions, then amplify them via social media, newsletters, or community events, demonstrating the effectiveness of compassionate communication and successful de-escalation.

Incorporating these stories into officer training emphasizes empathy and best practices, helping officers adopt approaches that are both compassionate and effective. Collaborations with autism organizations enhance this impact by providing officers with crucial insights, joint training opportunities, and resources that build understanding of sensory sensitivities and communication strategies.

These partnerships foster open dialogue, helping law enforcement develop informed responses in both routine and crisis situations, benefiting individuals on the autism spectrum. By participating in awareness campaigns and training initiatives, law enforcement strengthens community ties and shows a commitment to inclusivity, making individuals with autism and their families feel supported and respected. Ultimately, these efforts create a safer, more inclusive society for everyone.

Chapter 8

Legal Considerations

This framework for first responders regarding legal considerations in disability rights and autism awareness is critical for gaining trust and promoting proper interactions between first responders and individuals with disabilities. A clear understanding of disability rights not only ensures compliance with laws like the Americans with Disabilities Act (ADA) and Section 504 of the Rehabilitation Act but also enhances the quality of service provided by first responders. When first responders are equipped with the knowledge and tools to recognize, understand, and appropriately respond to individuals on the autism spectrum, it builds a foundation of trust within the community. This trust is essential, as it can significantly influence how individuals with disabilities and their families perceive and interact with first responders.

By integrating autism awareness into everyday first responders practices, they can prevent misunderstandings or unnecessary escalations that may arise due to misinterpreting behaviors linked to autism.

Properly accommodating the unique needs of autistic individuals, such as recognizing sensory sensitivities, non-verbal communication, or anxiety in unfamiliar environments, can lead to more effective and compassionate interactions. Moreover, by adhering to legal requirements and incorporating best practices for accommodating disabilities, first responders not only protect themselves from potential legal liabilities but also build a sense of inclusion, showing the community that they value the dignity and rights of all individuals.

Incorporating disability rights and autism awareness into first responders training ensures that they are prepared to handle diverse situations with empathy and professionalism. This proactive approach not only mitigates risks associated with civil rights violations but also enhances the reputation of first responders as inclusive and responsive entities that serve all members of the community equally. Furthermore, as first responders gain more experience in this area, their ability to de-escalate situations and engage effectively with individuals with autism becomes second nature, promoting safer and more positive outcomes during encounters.

In essence, embedding disability rights and autism awareness into first responders practices goes beyond mere legal compliance, it serves as a key driver in strengthening community relations, reducing the potential for conflict, and promoting public safety in a way that respects the diverse needs of all individuals.

Civil Rights Protections:

Individuals with autism are protected under several key civil rights laws that ensure their rights and prevent discrimination. The **Americans with Disabilities Act (ADA)** and **Section 504 of the Rehabilitation Act** are two foundational statutes that play a crucial role in safeguarding the rights of individuals with autism and other disabilities.

The **ADA** prohibits discrimination against individuals with disabilities in all areas of public life, including employment, education, transportation, and public accommodations. For first responders, this means they must ensure that individuals with autism have the same access to services and protections as anyone else. This includes making reasonable modifications in procedures, policies, and practices to prevent discrimination. For example, if a person with autism struggles to communicate verbally, first responders may need to provide alternative communication methods or allow extra time for the person to respond.

Section 504 of the Rehabilitation Act similarly prohibits discrimination on the basis of disability in programs and activities that receive federal financial assistance, including first responders. This law ensures that individuals with disabilities are not excluded from participating in, denied the benefits of, or subjected to discrimination in any program or activity that receives federal funding.

In practice, these civil rights protections require first responders to approach interactions with individuals with autism in a way that acknowledges their disability and respects their rights. This might mean modifying standard procedures during a traffic stop, investigation, or arrest to accommodate the individual's needs. Failure to adhere to these legal protections can result in legal consequences for both individual first responders and their departments, while compliance ensures fairness and equity, promoting better relations between first responders and the disability community.

Right to Accommodations:

Individuals with disabilities, including those with autism, have the legal right to receive **reasonable accommodations** in public settings under laws like the **Americans with Disabilities Act (ADA)**. This means that first responders must be prepared to adjust their standard procedures to meet the unique needs of individuals with autism in a fair and nondiscriminatory manner.

For people with autism, reasonable accommodations can take many forms. First responders may need to modify their communication approach, such as using simpler language, providing written instructions, or using visual aids for those who are non-verbal or have difficulty understanding verbal instructions. In certain situations, they might need to give the individual extra time to process information or respond, as quick decision-making or answering complex questions under pressure can be overwhelming for someone on the spectrum.

Additionally, accommodations could involve changes in how first responders interact physically. For example, an individual with autism might have heightened sensitivities to touch or loud sounds, so first responders may need to avoid physically restraining the person unless absolutely necessary or turn off flashing lights and sirens to reduce sensory overload. In some cases, it might be appropriate to call for support from a family member, caregiver, or specialized crisis response team familiar with autism.

Recognizing that every person with autism is different, accommodations must be flexible and tailored to the individual's specific needs. Failure to provide reasonable accommodations can not only escalate situations but may also violate the person's civil rights. On the other hand, understanding and implementing appropriate accommodations demonstrates respect for the person's dignity and rights, ensuring a more positive and effective interaction.

By adjusting their approach to accommodate these unique needs, first responders can de-escalate potentially challenging situations, avoid misunderstandings, and build trust with individuals on the autism spectrum and the broader disability community. This kind of awareness is critical in ensuring that individuals with autism are treated fairly and respectfully in public and legal interactions.

ADA Compliance and Regulations

Compliance with the Americans with Disabilities Act (ADA) is essential for first responders because it not only ensures that they uphold the civil rights of individuals with disabilities, but it also protects agencies from legal liability. The ADA mandates that individuals with disabilities, including those with autism, have equal access to public services, which includes First Responders. This means that all services, interactions, and facilities must be accessible to individuals with disabilities, whether that involves physical accommodations, like accessible police stations, or procedural accommodations, such as modifying communication methods or de-escalation tactics for people with sensory or cognitive challenges.

Failing to comply with the ADA can result in serious consequences, including lawsuits, financial penalties, and damage to the agency's reputation. Beyond the legal implications, ADA compliance is a vital component of fair and equitable policing, ensuring that first responders are trained to recognize and respond appropriately to individuals with disabilities. This compliance requires ongoing training, policy development, and an institutional commitment to inclusivity and equal treatment. By adhering to ADA guidelines, first responders demonstrate their commitment to serving and protecting all members of the community, including those with disabilities, in a way that is respectful, compassionate, and legally sound.

Access to Services:

First responders must ensure that all individuals, regardless of disability, have equal access to their services, in compliance with laws like the **Americans with Disabilities Act (ADA)**. This means that individuals with disabilities, including those with autism, should be able to access the same first responders services as anyone else, without facing barriers due to their condition.

Access includes both **physical access** and **communication access**. On the physical side, police stations, jails, and other first responders facilities must be designed or adapted to be accessible to people with mobility impairments. This could involve installing ramps, widening doorways, or providing accessible restrooms. Additionally, first responders vehicles or holding areas may need to accommodate individuals with physical disabilities.

Beyond physical access, **appropriate communication methods** are also essential. For individuals with autism or other cognitive or sensory disabilities, traditional forms of communication, such as spoken commands or written forms, may not always be effective. First responders need to be trained in alternative communication methods, which may include the use of sign language interpreters, picture exchange communication systems (PECS), or simply allowing more time for responses. Some individuals with autism may be non-verbal and rely on assistive devices to communicate, so first responders should be prepared to work with these technologies as well.

Providing **effective communication** may also involve modifying how first responders interact during interviews, interrogations, or when reading rights. For instance, a first responder may need to break down complex legal language into simpler terms or provide visual aids to help explain concepts to someone with cognitive disabilities. Ensuring access to services extends to responding appropriately in crisis situations, such as ensuring that first responders understand how to approach, de-escalate, and provide aid to individuals who may not communicate or behave in a typical manner due to their disability.

By ensuring both physical and communication access to services, first responders not only comply with the ADA but also create a more inclusive and supportive environment for all individuals in the community. This proactive approach prevents discrimination, fosters trust, and enhances public safety by ensuring that individuals with disabilities receive the services and protections to which they are entitled.

Training on ADA Regulations:

Providing comprehensive training on the Americans with Disabilities Act (ADA) is crucial for first responders to understand their legal responsibilities and interact appropriately with individuals with disabilities. This training should offer a foundational understanding of the ADA's purpose, prohibiting discrimination and ensuring equal access to public services, including first responders. Key areas of focus should include recognizing the signs of disabilities, particularly hidden or cognitive disabilities such as autism, and understanding what constitutes a reasonable accommodation. Additionally, the training should address the legal requirements of the ADA and the potential consequences of non-compliance, such as lawsuits or civil penalties, ensuring first responders are well-equipped to provide equitable and effective service.

What Constitutes a Reasonable Accommodation: First responders must be trained to understand what constitutes a reasonable accommodation in different situations. Reasonable accommodations are adjustments to standard practices or procedures that allow individuals with disabilities to access first responders services on equal footing with others. Examples might include allowing extra time for a person with autism to process information, adjusting communication methods (such as using written instructions or visual aids), or modifying physical interactions, such as avoiding handcuffing someone who has sensory sensitivities. Training should emphasize that accommodations are not about giving "special treatment" but about ensuring equal access to services.

Recognizing Signs of Disability: A critical aspect of ADA training is helping first responders recognize signs of disability, particularly when disabilities are not immediately obvious. For instance, individuals with autism may display behaviors such as avoiding eye contact, repetitive movements, difficulty following commands, or heightened sensitivity to sensory stimuli. Without proper training, first responders might misinterpret these behaviors as defiance, aggression, or resistance. Learning to recognize these signs will help first responders respond appropriately and avoid unnecessary escalation or the use of force.

Tailoring Responses to the Individual: Since disabilities affect individuals differently, first responders should be trained to approach each situation with flexibility. This may involve asking if the individual needs accommodations or adapting their approach on the spot. For example, in a crisis situation, first responders may need to reduce sensory triggers by turning off sirens or lights, or allow the individual more time to communicate their needs.

Crisis Intervention and De-escalation: ADA training should include strategies for de-escalating situations involving individuals with disabilities, particularly those with cognitive or sensory disabilities like autism. First responders should learn to use calm, clear communication, avoid quick movements or loud noises, and involve caregivers or crisis intervention teams if needed. Knowing how to approach someone in distress while providing reasonable accommodations can prevent misunderstandings and reduce the likelihood of an adverse outcome.

Ongoing Education and Refreshers: ADA regulations and best practices evolve over time, so first responders should receive ongoing training and refresher courses. These sessions can incorporate real-life case studies or examples of how ADA compliance has been successfully implemented, or overlooked, in first responders interactions.

By providing this training, administrators ensure that their staff not only comply with the ADA but are also better equipped to protect and serve all members of the community. This knowledge enhances the first responders ability to make informed decisions in real-time, reduces the risk of discrimination, and constructs more positive and respectful interactions with individuals with disabilities.

Detailed Incident Reports

Proper documentation is crucial for ensuring legal compliance, accountability, and effective communication among first responders. It serves as the foundation for transparent operations, providing reliable records of community interactions and supporting adherence to legal standards, such as the Americans with Disabilities Act (ADA). Detailed records demonstrate that first responders are fulfilling their obligations to treat individuals respectfully and offer necessary accommodations, helping protect against potential lawsuits and reinforcing public trust.

From an accountability standpoint, documentation allows first responders to track interactions, identify behavior patterns, and assess the effectiveness of training and policies. If reports reveal inadequate accommodations, agencies can revise training and improve practices, providing continuous improvement. Additionally, documentation acts as a feedback mechanism, enabling agencies to gather insights that allow updates to training, policies, and outreach efforts, ensuring a responsive approach to community needs.

Detailed incident reports are particularly vital when interacting with individuals on the autism spectrum. These reports serve as comprehensive records, capturing essential details about behaviors, communication methods, and accommodations provided. For example, first responders should document signs of anxiety, sensory overload, or other behavioral cues, as well as the communication strategies used, such as visual aids or simple language. Information about accommodations, like creating quieter environments or involving caregivers, emphasizes compliance with the ADA and commitment to equitable treatment.

Reports should also capture the outcomes of interactions, summarizing the actions taken, resolutions achieved, and the individual's response to accommodations. A review and feedback mechanism can identify trends and areas for improvement, integrating feedback from individuals with autism and their families. This allows agencies to continuously enhance their understanding and improve their responses.

Moreover, documentation facilitates communication between various units within first responder agencies and external stakeholders, such as supervisors, community organizations, and advocacy groups. Well-documented reports enhance collaboration and ensure that everyone is informed about the needs and experiences of individuals with disabilities, helping to develop tailored responses that uphold the rights of all individuals and improve public safety.

Timeliness in completing reports is also essential. As first responders, our memory is not infallible, and the details of an incident can fade quickly over time. The longer we wait to document an encounter, the more likely it is that important details will be forgotten or misremembered. By completing reports promptly, we ensure that the information captured is accurate and comprehensive, which is vital for maintaining legal compliance, accountability, and effective communication. Timely documentation also strengthens the quality of training and policy development by preserving the nuances of each interaction while they are still fresh in memory.

It is vital to remember, that proper documentation is more than a procedural requirement;

it is a cornerstone of first responder operations, ensuring legal compliance, accountability, and better community engagement. By prioritizing accurate, detailed incident reports, agencies can adopt a compassionate and informed approach that builds trust, improves understanding, and leads to better outcomes for individuals with autism.

Incorporate Feedback:

Incorporating feedback from individuals with disabilities and their families is crucial for enhancing the performance of first responders and identifying areas for improvement. This feedback provides unique insights into the effectiveness of interactions, allowing agencies to understand how well first responders apply autism awareness training and accommodations, and whether individuals feel respected and understood. To facilitate this, first responders should establish structured mechanisms for collecting feedback, such as post-incident surveys or feedback forms tailored to individuals with disabilities. Documenting this feedback meticulously in incident reports or tracking systems ensures that key insights are captured, highlighting appreciated aspects and any concerns raised.

Incorporating feedback into performance assessments, agencies can evaluate and enhance overall performance, identify trends, and determine if specific first responders need additional training. This practice promotes a culture of accountability and continuous improvement. Feedback also helps pinpoint specific areas in need of enhancement, such as communication methods or accommodations, enabling agencies to revise training programs and better serve individuals with disabilities. Actively seeking and utilizing feedback ensures community engagement and trust, encouraging further dialogue and collaboration. This open communication strengthens the relationship between first responders and the community, ultimately leading to more positive and effective interactions with individuals with disabilities.

Continuous training and development are essential for first responders to effectively support individuals with autism and other disabilities, guided by community feedback. By integrating feedback into training curricula, agencies can equip first responders with the necessary skills and knowledge for adaptive response strategies. This practice not only enhances their ability to respond but also establishes a culture of adaptability within first responder teams. In summary, using feedback from individuals with disabilities and their families in documentation processes is crucial for assessing performance and identifying areas for improvement, ultimately leading to more respectful and effective engagements with the community.

Maintaining comprehensive training records related to autism awareness and disability rights is vital for demonstrating compliance and a genuine commitment to addressing the unique needs of autistic individuals. Detailed records allow agencies to evaluate the effectiveness of training programs and inform curriculum development through a feedback loop that considers participant insights and real-world application outcomes. This process ensures that training remains impactful and evolves to meet the specific needs of both responders and the community.

Maintaining these records promotes accountability and transparency, reflecting the agency's dedication to professional development and public trust. Regular updates to training documents help identify the need for refresher sessions, ensuring that first responders are well-versed in best practices and legal requirements. Collaboration with advocacy organizations can be strengthened through shared training initiatives, enhancing resources and opportunities that bolster the abilities of first responders and benefit the wider community. This integrated approach ensures continuous improvement and preparedness in handling interactions with individuals on the autism spectrum effectively.

Conclusion:

In conclusion, a supportive environment for individuals with autism and other disabilities hinges on first responders understanding of legal considerations, including disability rights and compliance with the Americans with Disabilities Act (ADA). This knowledge is critical as it helps first responders navigate complex interactions while ensuring dignity and respect for all individuals, ensuring equal rights and protections under the law. When well-versed in these legal frameworks, first responders can proactively manage and de-escalate potential issues, reducing misunderstandings or conflicts. Implementing best practices for documentation further supports accountability and effectiveness. Thorough records of interactions provide valuable insights into performance and contribute to continuous improvement by refining training programs and adapting policies based on feedback. This commitment to understanding and accountability not only benefits individuals with autism but enhances community safety and well-being, building trust and cooperation. Ultimately, by prioritizing legal awareness, meticulous documentation, and ongoing training, first responders create a more inclusive environment that positively impacts individuals with disabilities and the community at large.

Chapter 9

Every Call Counts: Why Training Never Stops

In the field of law enforcement, the ability to protect and serve is not limited to enforcing laws or responding to crises. At the heart of this duty lies a critical skill that transcends physical tactics and even the most advanced tools of our trade: communication. As first responders, we are often faced with situations where our words and actions can either escalate or de-escalate a situation, and this is especially true when interacting with individuals on the autism spectrum. As a father to a nonverbal child with autism, I've come to understand firsthand the importance of effective communication. Even after years of experience, I am still learning new strategies to better support my daughter, and others like her. This ongoing learning process is not just valuable; it is vital.

It is easy to assume that once we've acquired a certain set of skills or knowledge, our training is complete. However, when it comes to autism awareness and de-escalation techniques, the truth is, there is no finish line. The journey is ongoing, and continued training is the key to ensuring that we, as first responders, are best equipped to handle the complex and sometimes delicate situations that arise when interacting with individuals with autism.

This leads me to an experience I had while teaching an autism awareness class to my department. I remember that after completing my first year of teaching this subject, numerous officers approached me to share their thoughts and feelings. Many of these officers were seasoned veterans with more than 20 years of experience, and nearly all of them said the same thing: "If only I knew then what I know now."

They would go on to recount incidents they had encountered many years ago, often recalling the details from the incident. As they described how they handled those calls, some expressed gratitude, feeling they had made the right decisions despite limited knowledge at the time. Others, however, were visibly disappointed in themselves, lamenting the choices they had made and wishing they had approached the situation differently. Their reflections underscored how much they had learned and how they now recognized opportunities they had missed to better serve the individuals involved.

I recall a vital conversation with a buddy of mine from the fire department. Out of curiosity, I asked him what type of training they receive on autism. His response left me stunned: "Whatever the previous call we went on, where the patient was autistic." He went on to clarify, explaining that they don't receive any formal autism training. Their entire philosophy, he said, was essentially, "If it worked last time, let's try it this time."

This approach, while practical in the moment, highlights a glaring gap in preparation and understanding. Without dedicated training, first responders risk relying on trial and error, which can lead to inconsistent and potentially harmful outcomes. Each individual with autism is unique, and what works in one situation may not be effective, or even appropriate, in another.

Training is not just a box to check; it is vital for all first responders to better themselves and serve their communities with competence and compassion. Proper education equips them with the tools to handle complex and sensitive situations, ensuring they can provide the best possible care and support to those in need. For first responders to truly fulfill their mission, continuous learning must be prioritized as a cornerstone of their service.

For any officer to say they don't need to learn more is to do a disservice to the public and the people they serve. There is always room for growth, and these conversations with my colleagues were a powerful testament to that truth. Their willingness to acknowledge past shortcomings and embrace new understanding proved that we are never above our training. It also reinforced the importance of continuous learning in our profession, not just for the sake of doing our job better, but for the lives we touch in every interaction.

A Personal Perspective: The Need for Continuous Learning

As a father, I have often reflected on past situations with my daughter, wondering how different things might have been if I had known what I know

now. Autism is a vast spectrum, and my daughter's needs and responses are unique. But through years of experience, research, and collaboration with experts in the field, I've learned strategies that have dramatically improved my ability to connect with her. And yet, I recognize that I am still learning, both from her and from others in the autism community.

When I look back at certain situations, especially those where I struggled to understand her behavior or needs, I realize, had I been better equipped with the knowledge and strategies that I have now, I might have approached things differently. Whether it was using more effective communication techniques, recognizing sensory overloads sooner, or offering her a calm environment to help mitigate her anxiety, there are countless opportunities where continued learning could have made a difference. And this is precisely why continued training for first responders is so crucial.

The stakes are incredibly high. When law enforcement officers interact with individuals on the autism spectrum, we must understand that their responses to stress, communication, and sensory input can be very different from what we are used to. Without proper training, our responses can unintentionally escalate a situation, making it harder to de-escalate and potentially leading to harmful outcomes. By constantly refining our understanding of autism, we can better serve the individuals in our community who are often the most vulnerable, including those with autism, their families, and anyone else who may be impacted by our actions.

The Duty to Protect: Why Continued Training is Essential

As first responders, we have a duty and an obligation to protect the public to the best of our ability. This duty does not stop with standard law enforcement training, which may focus heavily on firearms, tactics, and physical response. While these are undoubtedly important aspects of the job, they should not be the only areas where we focus our time and effort. If we are truly dedicated to protecting and serving everyone in our communities, we must invest in the education and training that will help us engage with all individuals, especially those who are neurodivergent or have other special needs.

There is nothing more that we want then the public to trust us to be calm, patient, and professional when interacting with vulnerable populations, including individuals with autism. When these interactions turn into crises, we must be equipped to communicate effectively and de-escalate, not only to protect the individual we're interacting with but also to protect ourselves and our fellow responders. If we are not constantly evolving our understanding of autism and how it impacts behavior, we risk losing opportunities for peaceful resolutions and may inadvertently cause harm.

The Importance of Teamwork and Preparation: A Mindset Shift

As law enforcement officers, we are constantly faced with new challenges, some of which require quick, decisive action. However, I know an officer I worked with who has repeatedly told me, when I asked him to sign up for an active shooter training, that he didn't see the need, stating it's just an active shooter and he would "just respond" when the time came. This mentality, reflects a dangerous mindset that can jeopardize not only the officer's safety but the safety of the community and other first responders that serve with him.

This approach overlooks the crucial role that preparation and collaboration play in any response, no matter the situation's intensity. It's not enough to simply "respond" when the time comes. Law enforcement is about learning how to work together as a team, honing skills that allow us to assess, adapt, and communicate effectively, regardless of whether the situation is an emergency or routine.

The importance of continuous training and collaboration extends far beyond rare events like active shooter scenarios. In fact, it's critical for everyday situations that we face as first responders. Think back to how many times we've conducted traffic stops during our training or how often we've responded to family disturbances in the academy. How long did we spend in field training, learning from veteran first responders, refining our communication skills, and adapting our responses to a wide variety of real-life situations? That time spent honing our skills is invaluable. It's what shapes us into competent, confident first responders who know how to assess a situation and make the right call. Whether that's de-escalating a potentially violent confrontation, recognizing signs of distress in an individual, or effectively communicating in a high-pressure environment.

This training is not just about "showing up" or reacting in the moment; it's about preparing ourselves mentally, physically, and emotionally for a variety of situations. The better we prepare and practice working together, the more confident and effective we will be in the field. Whether it's handling a crisis with an individual on the autism spectrum or managing a routine traffic stop, our ability to work together and rely on our training can make all the difference.

The Power of Communication: Our Most Important Tool

Throughout my career, I've learned one of the most powerful tools we have as first responders is our ability to communicate. I can't count the number of times I successfully de-escalated a situation simply by taking a moment to speak clearly, listen actively, and respond with empathy. And this skill has proven invaluable in my personal life as well. With my own daughter, I have learned that communication is not just about words. It's about understanding nonverbal cues, being patient, and adjusting my approach to meet her needs.

In the field, the situations I've faced have often been tense, with high emotions and pressure to act quickly. In these moments, it's not enough to rely solely on physical tactics or protocols. The ability to speak calmly, to listen attentively, and to use de-escalation strategies can make all the difference. I've seen firsthand how much can be accomplished through simple, thoughtful communication. Yet, these moments of success didn't happen by chance, they happened because of the training I had received. These experiences are reminders that effective communication isn't just a skill we learn once and use forever; it's a skill we must continue to refine.

For example, there have been instances where I've interacted with individuals on the autism spectrum, and because of the communication strategies I had learned, I was able to avoid unnecessary confrontation and ensure a peaceful resolution. Had I not been trained or had my own experiences in autism awareness or de-escalation techniques, these situations might have ended very differently. The knowledge I gained through ongoing training gave me the tools I needed to recognize the signs of distress, adjust my communication style, and create a safe environment where the person could feel heard and respected.

Continued Training: A Necessity for Growth

The reality is that continued training isn't just about learning new techniques, it's about ensuring growth, both personally and professionally. We are all evolving in our understanding of autism and neurodiversity, and as we learn, we become better equipped to make decisions that prioritize safety and understanding.

Law enforcement, like any profession, evolves over time. New research, best practices, and real-world experiences emerge, and if we are committed to improving our ability to serve our communities, we must be committed to continuous learning. In the case of autism, this means staying informed about the latest research, learning from those who experience autism firsthand, and understanding the unique needs and challenges that individuals on the spectrum face daily.

As we continue our education, we also strengthen the bond between law enforcement and the community. By demonstrating a commitment to understanding empathy, we not only improve our interactions with individuals with autism but also with their families, friends, and the wider community. This engagement fosters trust, promotes inclusivity, and ensures that our communities feel safe, valued, and understood.

Conclusion: The Lifelong Commitment to Learning

For first responders, continued training is not optional, it's a moral obligation. As I reflect on my own experiences, both as a law enforcement officer and as a father, I recognize the profound impact that continued education can have. By committing ourselves to lifelong learning, we ensure that we are always prepared to protect, serve, and communicate effectively with everyone, including those with autism. This commitment not only strengthens our professional skills but also enriches our understanding, making us more compassionate, more effective, and better equipped to meet the needs of all individuals, regardless of their neurological makeup. The better we understand autism, the better we can serve those who need our help the most.

In the end, it's not about how we respond when everything is going right, it's about how we manage ourselves and our reactions when things are going wrong. This is what makes ongoing training so essential. The more we learn about different conditions, the more we understand the behaviors and struggles that people in crisis may face. And the more we practice de-escalation techniques, the better equipped we are to handle situations with patience, empathy, and professionalism. We have a duty to protect everyone we encounter, and this includes understanding how best to support those who might need a different kind of help.

I once heard an important truth for us responders to remember, "just because you attend a training once in your life, doesn't make you an expert." This is an important truth for us as responders to remember. Thinking about the knowledge I have as a first responder and with autism, I still learn new things every day. Training is not a one-time event; it is an ongoing process of growth and improvement. Just like any skill, our ability to handle crisis situations, especially those involving individuals with autism or other mental health conditions, improves with continuous practice and learning. The more training we seek out, the more tools we add to our toolbox, the more knowledgeable and understanding we get at responding to the needs of those in crisis, the better our response will be. As the world around us evolves, so too must our approach to serving and protecting those we encounter.

The Road Ahead: Embracing the Unknown

As I reflect on my years as a first responder and a father to a non-verbal autistic child, I realize how deeply these experiences have shaped my life and inspired this book. Every challenge, every breakthrough, and every moment of connection with my daughter has led me to this point. The lessons I've learned through my family have been invaluable, teaching me that family always comes first, no matter the circumstances. It's increasingly vital for all first responders to understand that, within the system, we are often just a number to our agencies. Do not forget it is our family that remains our true source of loyalty, love, and support. Our commitment to them should always take precedence, for they are the ones who will stand by us when everything else fades.

The passion behind this book is rooted in my unwavering commitment to both my family and the greater community. My journey has not been without its struggles, but each difficulty has been met with determination, love, and an unyielding belief in the power of understanding. I am grateful for the growth that has come from these experiences, knowing that each day brings new milestones, successes, and challenges to overcome.

The unknowns ahead, whether they be struggles, triumphs, or unexpected moments of grace, continue to fuel my purpose. I am driven by the desire to bridge the gap between first responders and the autism community, to build a more inclusive world where every individual is seen, heard, and understood. My family has been my guide, my inspiration, and my heart through it all, and it is through their strength that I am able to move forward with hope and conviction.

This book is only the beginning of that journey, a testament to the power of love, understanding, and the commitment to making a difference in the lives of those who need it most.

As I reflect on all that has brought me here, I am filled with deep gratitude for my family and our sweet Lilian, whose presence in our family has been a constant reminder of the power of love, resilience, and belonging. Lilian, thank you for trusting us to raise you, for showing us every day how to embrace the beauty of your unique spirit. You are our heart, and your journey is our journey, as it shapes us in ways words cannot fully express. We promise to always be by your side, to support you through every challenge, celebrate every success, and honor every milestone. To the autism community, we stand with you in solidarity, committed to building a world where every individual is seen, heard, and loved for who they are.

Only together can we grow, as first responders and the autism community, standing strong side by side, piece by piece, like a puzzle coming together.

Made in the USA
Columbia, SC
13 February 2025